Please return/renew this item by the last date shown. Books may also be renewed by phone or internet.

 www3.rbwm.gov.uk/libraries

☎ 01628 796969 (library hours)

☎ 0303 123 0035 (24 hours)

www.rbwm.gov.uk

Royal Borough of Windsor & Maidenhead

Windsor and Maidenhead

THE
EX MEN

THE
EX MEN

HOW OUR FORMER PRESIDENTS AND PRIME MINISTERS ARE STILL CHANGING THE WORLD

GILES EDWARDS

Biteback Publishing

First published in Great Britain in 2020 by
Biteback Publishing Ltd, London
Copyright © Giles Edwards 2020

ISBN 978-1-84954-770-3

10 9 8 7 6 5 4 3 2 1

A CIP catalogue record for this book is available from the British Library.

Set in Minion Pro

Printed and bound in Great Britain by
CPI Group (UK) Ltd, Croydon CR0 4YY

For my parents, Sue and Charles Edwards, with love,
admiration and enormous gratitude.

CONTENTS

INTRODUCTION

'How come when someone loses power, that person also loses the meaning of life? How come power has such charisma for some people that its loss means the collapse of that person's world?'
PLAYWRIGHT AND FORMER CZECH PRESIDENT VÁCLAV HAVEL
SPEAKING AT THE OPENING OF HIS PLAY *LEAVING* IN PRAGUE,
21 MAY 2008[1]

One afternoon in April 2020, as British Prime Minister Boris Johnson returned to work after a spell in hospital with Covid-19, my wife turned to me and asked, 'Do you think Theresa May, or Tony Blair, or Gordon Brown, would want to be Prime Minister now?' It's an excellent question. The scale of the challenge presented to a national leader by the coronavirus pandemic is dazzling: uncertain, fantastically complicated, and with tremendous risk to livelihoods and even the lives of your citizens. And the outcomes depend, far more than normal government decisions, on the Prime Minister taking the right decisions. It's enough to put most people off – but of course we're not talking about most people. We're talking about the men and women whose combination of skills, expertise, dynamism, charisma, good health, good luck and self-belief got them to the very top of politics. And those qualities don't desert

1

them once they leave office. And so at this most challenging moment here's former Prime Minister Gordon Brown, coordinating open letters from a veritable who's who of the political and economic great and good, from dozens of different countries, calling for more effective global responses. There's former Prime Minister Theresa May, urging governments worldwide to stop seeing purely national solutions to the pandemic.[2] And everywhere there's former Prime Minister Tony Blair: popping up to argue for a reorganisation of the British government to cope with the pandemic, announcing that his own organisation will refocus completely on the coronavirus and its consequences, and urging a stronger World Health Organization (WHO). 'Tony Blair is having a Covid moment,' noted *The Economist*, drily.[3] On the other side of the Atlantic, America's former leaders are partying like it's 1999, too. Former US President Bill Clinton is refocusing his work on the response to Covid-19, using his annual summit to press governors of major US states to establish an effective tracing programme once the peak has passed. His successor, George W. Bush, releases a video calling for Americans to come together and set partisan differences aside.

And as I survey all this, I ponder that question: would these men and women who have been at the very top of government, including during times of grave national emergencies, secretly rather like to be running the show again? Are they looking at the current leaders – Boris Johnson and Donald Trump – and thinking, 'I can do better than that' or 'Go on, let me have a go'? Or are they happy – and how you see this will very much depend on your perspective – to offer their nations the benefit of their wisdom and experience, or to carp from the side-lines? This book doesn't offer an answer to the first question, but it does try to answer the second – what they are and aren't happy to do. A couple of weeks before that question from my wife, as the pandemic was just beginning to hit Europe, I spoke to Mary Robinson, the then 75-year-old former Irish President, who, since leaving office, has never been less than fantastically busy. It's an example she imbibed from her father: in her memoirs she quotes him saying that it was 'better to wear out than rust out'.[4] And when I asked her how she copes, and why at her age she carries on at such a pace, she told me she's actually feeling driven to do more, not less.

> I think it's because I have an increasing sense of urgency, basic-ally … We are not on course for a safe world for our children and grandchildren. Nick [her husband] and myself, we happen to have six lovely grandchildren, from sixteen to two. They'll share a world in 2050 with far more people, it's estimated maybe 9.5 billion. How will that world feed itself? How will there be any kind of social order in that world unless we take steps now, which we're not taking?

Since her time as President of Ireland, Robinson has been the United Nations High Commissioner for Human Rights, she's run two of her own non-governmental organisations (NGOs) and ad-vised numerous others and she chairs a team of former Presidents called The Elders. And of course she's not the only one. Gordon Brown has taken on a significant UN role; Bill Clinton runs his own highly successful foundation; George W. Bush works with the mil-itary veterans whose lives are so intertwined with the decisions he took while President. And Tony Blair? Well…

• • •

Blair actually has answered the first question – about whether he'd like to be Prime Minister again. In 2012, five years after he left

Downing Street, Sarah Sands of the *Evening Standard* asked him straight. 'Yes, sure, but it's not likely to happen is it?' he replied.[5] To anyone watching Tony Blair, that can hardly have come as a surprise, because after he stood down as Prime Minister he appears to have modelled his new life on his old one, just without the inconvenient faff of accountability and press scrutiny. He set up a myriad of companies and foundations: the Tony Blair Sports Foundation, the Tony Blair Faith Foundation, the Africa Governance Initiative, Tony Blair Associates. He took on a major international role – as Envoy for the so-called Quartet in the Middle East peace process, a job he handled, according to his biographer John Rentoul, like he thought he was working for peace in Northern Ireland again.* Even his office on the corner of London's Grosvenor Square had echoes of 10 Downing Street: walking in, it was hard not to be struck by the similarity in the set-up. Between them, this web of organisations allowed Blair to continue working on any policy issue which interested him, speak out on questions of faith and continue hobnobbing with serving heads of state and government. It helped Blair that his successor, Gordon Brown, had an uneven start to his premiership. Ten months in, Labour peer Lord Desai spoke for many when he quipped that 'Gordon Brown was put on earth to remind people how good Tony Blair was'.[6] A few weeks after that and Blair was gracing *Time* magazine's list of the world's 100 most influential people, an honour never accorded him while serving as Prime Minister.[7] He put himself in the running to be the first President of the European Council of the European Union, was awarded the Presidential Medal of Freedom by George W. Bush (America's highest civilian honour) and, as he travelled around the world, particularly the Middle East in his

---

* The Quartet is made up of the European Union, United Nations, United States and Russia.

capacity as Quartet Envoy, scooped up a series of other awards and degrees – and paid consulting gigs.

And here's where Blair the former Prime Minister, a man who first entered No. 10 on a wave of commitment to open government, with promises to end the culture of 'sleaze' and a borderline obsession with image, has stumbled. There are two broad interpretations of Blair's money-making, which until 2016 ran to millions of pounds every year, from the usual speechifying and advisory work for corporate giants like JP Morgan and Zurich Financial Services to advising authoritarian rulers like then President of Kazakhstan Nursultan Nazarbayev. The first interpretation is that there's nothing wrong with Blair using his 'prestige and personal contacts' to make money, some of which is then funnelled into his philanthropic foundations.[8] The second is that this is unseemly for a former Prime Minister; that Blair has consistently muddied the waters between his philanthropic, business and diplomatic interests, deliberately setting up a fabulously complex web of companies to hide the amount and sources of his earnings, and leaving even neutral observers asking, 'Why do that if you have nothing to hide?' The second interpretation has dominated, with the relatively small band of Tony Blair watchers dominated by those scrutinising his business interests.[9] In fact, so dominant has this narrative become for Blair that in 2016, when WikiLeaks published hacked emails relating to the Clinton Foundation, they revealed Bill Clinton's daughter Chelsea expressing considerable concern that the behaviour of some Clinton Foundation staff led to people in London 'making comparisons between my father and Tony Blair's profit motivations. Which would horrify my father.'[10] It's not the first time I've seen unfavourable comparisons between the Clinton and Blair fundraising machines, and, whatever the truth, the perception that Blair is motivated by money, and that he's raised it in disreputable ways, has been deeply harmful for his reputation. For those who admire Blair, including his largely sympathetic biographer John Rentoul, this is enormously frustrating. 'The fundamental problem is he's a very proud man,' Rentoul told me. 'When he stepped down, he thought, "I've had enough of this shit" and stopped caring about the very basics of public relations for his image, and it was very damaging for him.' What's more, this wave of negative coverage has largely obscured what Blair has done with the money. Over the years this has included a vast array of projects in Africa – particularly focused on governance – which speedily transferred into countering the 2014–16 Ebola epidemic. Assessments of the substance of his work as Quartet Envoy vary: he was criticised in many quarters for not achieving Middle East peace, for spending too much time with trifling details, but his remit was to promote Palestinian economic activity, and he had some success in assisting the Palestinian government and people to kickstart their economy, until the peace process broke down.

At the end of 2016, almost ten years after he left office and in the wake of the Brexit referendum and the election of Donald Trump in the United States, Blair took stock of his sprawling network. He'd already left his role as Quartet Envoy, and decided it was time to close his businesses and foundations, consolidating all his work under one roof, in the not-for-profit Tony Blair Institute for Global Change. It appeared to be an admission, in part, that some of his judgements had been faulty: in announcing the changes, he noted that his business work had been 'open to misrepresentation and to criticism either that we were conflating private and public roles or that we were working in countries which aroused controversy'. 'I have learnt a huge amount about the world and frankly what I can do and can't do to affect it positively,' he continued, perhaps an acknowledgement that it was time to jettison that sense of 'I've had enough of this shit', as John Rentoul put it. The taking stock included a new and narrower focus – on governance, extremism, Israeli–Palestinian peace, and countering populism – and it would be much more open about its priorities, people and finances.

It remains to be seen whether this transformation will improve his image enough to persuade people to listen again to what he has to say. For many people, the combination of his dash for cash and his record in government, and in particular his decision to take Britain into war in Iraq, can never be forgiven. As journalist Alex Perry wrote in 2015, having travelled with Blair, including to those Ebola hotspots in the midst of the epidemic,

> Blair's name is a headline swearword and a Pavlovian trigger for many normally level-headed Brits to froth at the mouth ... Blair is the focus for a kind of righteous hate speech. Many Britons consider him to be a Machiavel with a Messiah complex, a war criminal who claims – the deviousness of the man! – to be saving the world.[11]

But perhaps the Covid-19 crisis is an opportunity for those still open-minded about Tony Blair to reconsider his post-premiership. At the start of 2020, his institute was working with the governments of fourteen sub-Saharan African countries, with a third of his staff spread across the continent, from Kenya in the east to Senegal in the west, Ethiopia in the north to Mozambique in the south. Working directly with Presidents and Prime Ministers, as well as other parts of the public sector, they were advising on a variety of projects, but a glance at the 2018 report suggests a couple of common themes.

First, supporting heads of government to drive through the kinds of changes they want to see. Blair's memoirs are full of stories of his own frustration at his inability to get the kind of change he wanted in Britain, and he's clearly exporting those lessons (basically: set up a delivery unit) to Africa.[12] Second, helping with private sector development, whether that's negotiating better deals or connecting with potential investors. Blair himself maintains relationships with the heads of government, and his teams were already embedded, relationships of trust already developed, when the Covid-19 pandemic hit. That is a phenomenal platform from which to pivot to supporting some of the world's poorest nations to deal with an unprecedented set of challenges.

So why the change from the previous arcane set of organisations? Well, although he has been careful to make clear that this is not a platform for some kind of attempted return to the political stage, Blair has hinted at one driver. 'I care about my country and the world my children and grandchildren will grow up in,' he wrote in that statement, 'and want to play at least a small part in contributing to the debate about the future of both.' It has strong echoes of Mary Robinson, doesn't it? Perhaps it's partly that he's made enough money to, in his words, 'help with the funding to grow the organisations', and they're now sustainable. Perhaps he's made enough money himself and doesn't need any more – a potential rebuttal to that line from Chelsea Clinton about 'Tony Blair's profit motivations'. And perhaps it's something simpler: that since he retired as Prime Minister Tony Blair has wanted to use his contacts and experience, earned so painfully, to do good in the world. Most likely, of course, it's a bit of all of the above – although how you assess the exact balance will depend on how triggered you are by the thought that Blair could be trying to do the right thing. So Tony

Blair's 'Covid moment', to use *The Economist*'s words, might just be his coming-out (again) party.

Because Blair is such a fascinating figure, there has been a tendency in recent years to look at his post-premiership and think of him as a singular figure – that this portfolio career he has carved out for himself is unique. On this reading, it should come as no surprise that Blair's extraordinary energy and ability have been combined to such effect after office. But to think that way is to get Tony Blair, and what he represents, all wrong. For Blair's story is singular only in its scale; in every other respect it is part of a major and seriously under-reported development in recent history.

• • •

For many years, the idea of an unseen force – working alongside and between government, corporations and NGOs, wielding power in our world, for good or for evil – has captivated the public imagination. For the most part, this idealised third force has bounced between Peter Parker's Spider-Man and Diana Prince's Wonder Woman, and back again via the X-Men's Charles Xavier. But in the real world, the debate about who wields power has always remained disappointingly focused on governments and corporations (with the conspiracy theorist's gaze occasionally alighting on supra-national government, NGOs or the media). The truth, though, is that an extra, unseen group of people does exist – of a kind. They aren't quite in the same league as Wonder Woman, Spider-Man or the X-Men, but they do share some qualities with any good Marvel superhero. Like Diana Prince, they are hidden in plain sight. Like Peter Parker, they do have sometimes superhuman powers (although in a nod towards the humdrum these tend towards outsize personal qualities rather than extraordinary physical characteristics). And like Charles Xavier's X-Men they often work together in teams with complementary powers. Everyone knows they exist, but what few have known – until now – is how powerful they have become and how much they still affect the rest of us.

These are the men and women who, like Tony Blair, Bill Clinton, Gordon Brown and Mary Robinson, used to run a country – our former Presidents and Prime Ministers. And, like them, after leaving office they continue to roam the globe, consulting, lobbying, pressing, cajoling, speaking – still engaged, still active and still powerful. What makes them so intriguing is that while we all know their names and still receive occasional glimpses of what they do, in truth we know almost nothing about how they spend most of their time, and how much they still affect how we spend ours. With the exceptions of Blair, Brown and Clinton, they rarely grace our front pages these days, but that doesn't mean that these former leaders disappear off into obscurity. Most got to the top of their countries' greasy political poles the hard way, fought hard to stay there and don't much relish sliding back to the bottom again. What's more, they find that the personality traits that got them there and the expertise and contacts they acquired in the job – they remain gregarious, outgoing, knowledgeable deal-makers – remain much in demand. So instead of returning to normality, they instead stick at the top and begin their new lives, or what Fernando Henrique Cardoso, the former Brazilian President, calls their third career. Welcome to the world of the Ex Men.

• • •

To the untrained eye, those new lives, these third careers, can look an awful lot like the ones they've just left behind: the same private jets, the same round-the-clock security, the same warm welcome from their friends in high places, and the same summits and global meetings they used to attend (while a select few, like Bill Clinton, even manage to create their own global summits). So these Ex Men are not former leaders in any meaningful sense, merely former heads of state or government. But the difference from their former lives, what really makes them an outside, hidden force, is crucial. This new world involves no awkward accountability to voters or tiresome need to answer to the media. Instead, it offers the welcome opportunity to get things done, earn some money (sometimes a lot of money) or rehabilitate an image. But what are they getting done? What are they sacrificing along the way? Whose money are they taking and what are they offering in return? These are crucial questions, with few answers. And because of three developments that have swept the globe over the past fifty years, making this a unique moment in history for the number, variety and influence of the Ex Men, we need answers to these questions more urgently than ever before.

The first of these developments is the spread of democracy. You don't need to buy Francis Fukuyama's theory about the triumph of liberal democracy to agree that the history of the past fifty years has often been about its spread around the world. More democracies means two things. One: quite a lot of old dictators have been shunted out of presidential palaces. Two: more elections mean more democratic leaders turned out of office, which means more Ex Men. The second global development has been the burgeoning cult of youth, which over the past fifty years has affected politics in almost every country. Combined with the democratic revolution, this has changed the demographic profile of the Ex Men: generally, they are leaving office younger than their predecessors. Mary

Robinson left office at fifty-three, Bill Clinton and Tony Blair aged fifty-four, and Barack Obama at fifty-five. No wonder Fernando Henrique Cardoso, an active and influential Ex Man despite leaving office in Brazil aged seventy-one, sees full and fulfilling third careers beckoning for his younger colleagues. If the first development is about supply and the second about the type of supply, the third – globalisation – is about demand. The past half-century has seen a surge in the number of international organisations, multinational corporations, international charities and NGOs, not to mention dramatically simpler international travel and communication. The result is that everyone from the UN to the African Union, from CARE International to The Elders, and from Rosneft to Goldman Sachs are desperate for just the type of connections, expertise and drive the Ex Men have spent half a lifetime developing.

Getting into bed with existing power structures and big organisations like these is the most important way in which these olds hands get to stay in the game. It's often first on the to-do list for a newly minted Ex Man. But it's far from the only way, and there are so many opportunities available that this third career now almost has its own career structure. Next on the list is usually setting up your own foundation, which provides office space, a fundraising base and a purpose (the last can often be the most important when you've lost office – Jack McConnell, former First Minister of Scotland, told me that as a way of counteracting his disappointment and loss of purpose after leaving office, he changed the start-up screen on his mobile phone so it would tell him he was 'lucky, not unlucky' every time he switched it on). Depending on their international stature and the vigour of their country's publishing industry, around this time an Ex Man may also be deciding between several offers to write their memoirs, a valuable chance to earn some money, reset their image in the public mind, and think through their time in office. With the memoirs out of the way, the next task on an Ex Man's to-do list is to join some clubs: they now have several to choose from. But for all these ways to stay in the game, for many leaders the easiest way to retain influence is to maintain a position of political leadership in their own countries. This book isn't concerned with those Ex Men who remain involved in party politics, but beyond that they can usually expect access to the media, to politicians of their own party and, depending on the political circumstances, a hearing from the current political leaders, even if they are of another party. Business and non-governmental leaders are often happy to be called in to brief or for consultation, too – what former Canadian Prime Minister Kim Campbell calls her 'convening power'.

Perhaps you're wondering whether this is real power? Well, it's access, and the potential to influence, to persuade. I've always thought that the late Harvard academic Richard Neustadt's brilliant analysis of American presidential power – that 'the power of a President is the power to persuade' – is amongst the most insightful analyses of all power in politics. In fact, some leaders who have no large-p power at all, like Michael, the former King of Romania, whom I met in his home in the hills above Lake Geneva and about whom you'll hear more in Chapter 7, accumulated a lot of what another great Harvard mind, Joseph Nye, calls 'soft power'. Whether they are able to wield it effectively is another matter, and so over the past twelve years I've spent time with dozens of Ex Men and the people who work with – and sometimes against – them, to find out how they do it and what effect it has on our lives.

And since none of the things they get up to, and none of the organisations involved – from the organs of international government like the United Nations, the European Union, the North Atlantic

Treaty Organization (NATO) and the World Trade Organization to international NGOs, private foundations and multinational corporations – are exactly famed for their transparency and accountability, I think it's about time some light was shone in some of these dark corners, too. So I've quizzed them about their dealings and their new-found freedom from scrutiny, and poked around inside their organisations. I've been speaking to the people who hire them, and to the administrators and money men – people like Sir Richard Branson, the brains (and the money) behind The Elders, the late former South African President Nelson Mandela's old boys' club. I've talked to people who are concerned about their wielding of power, about their influence, and I've put those arguments directly to the Ex Men.

And what I've found is that these apparently Ex Men do still wield significant, and sometimes unexpected, influence on the world around us. Fernando Henrique Cardoso told me how he and some fellow Ex Men from Latin America set out to change the continent's discussion about drug laws – something he freely acknowledged he could never have done in office. Former US Ambassador Charles Stith, who studies African presidential leadership, explained to me that building respect for the men who have previously held the presidency is a powerful way of embedding these institutions in newly democratic societies. And F. W. de Klerk, the Nobel Laureate and former South African President, described to me how Ex Men, used for moral support and as informal sounding boards behind the scenes, can really help democratic leaders facing horrible decisions.

Of course, not every Ex Man has the opportunity to establish a foundation and pitch up on the speaking circuit. Some, like former Nigerian President Olusegun Obasanjo, spend time in jail on politically motivated charges. Others, like former Prime Ministers Silvio

Berlusconi of Italy or Ehud Olmert of Israel, have faced more transparent legal processes. Others still, like former Presidents Alberto Fujimori of Peru and Charles Taylor of Liberia, have been prosecuted in domestic courts or at international tribunals for serious human rights violations. Yet even many of these characters, the put-upon and the less savoury alike, continue to play major roles in their countries' politics – and sometimes those of the region. In Peru, Fujimori's family drama has been entwined with his country's modern history in the most extraordinary, and destructive, way; in Thailand, years of political turmoil have revolved around a former Prime Minister, Thaksin Shinawatra, who last held office in September 2006. Both men remain important figures in their country's politics, while Ex Men in countries from Poland to Pakistan similarly play a major role, whether as rallying points for opposition or as representatives in the public psyche of a bygone era of certainty and relative stability.

But something else has happened in the lives of these Ex Men since I first started working on this book. The values that underpinned the world order then – liberalism, a belief in democracy, and rules-based globalisation – have come under attack, and in a variety of ways. Whether that's from an expansionist China little interested in liberalism or democracy, from a newly assertive Russia seemingly little interested in a rules-based global order, or from Presidents in countries as varied as Brazil, Turkey and the United States who are very much focused on putting their countries' interests first, and less concerned about fraying notions of global solidarity or internationalism. It's a sign of the times that when George W. Bush released his video calling on Americans to come together and put aside partisan divisions during the Covid-19 crisis – little more than bland do-goodery at any normal time – it was regarded by President Trump as thinly veiled criticism. 'I appreciate the message from former President Bush, but where was he during Impeachment calling for putting partisanship aside. He was nowhere to be found in speaking up against the greatest Hoax in American history,' he rage-tweeted, referring to the impeachment hearings.

But the Ex Men are different. Their generation of leaders literally created the liberal, democratic and rules-based global order which is currently under attack. And as I've met them, and talked to them, it's very clear that their values haven't shifted. Instead, many of them are using third careers, in part, to fight for that world and those values.

• • •

In his memoirs, former Canadian Prime Minister Paul Martin describes his career since leaving office as 'post-political', 'post-public' and 'post-prime ministerial'. Of the three, only the third is really true, because like most Ex Men, while he has chosen his issues very carefully, his interventions have at times been both extremely political and highly public. This issue of what to call former Presidents and Prime Ministers is a common conundrum. Another popular name for them is 'former leaders': as I hope I will persuade you, that title could not be further from the truth. And so I've chosen to call them Ex Men. It's not perfect, either, because of the gender connotations, and I apologise for that and hope you can see past it (anyone who has watched the movies or read the comics will know there are many female X-Men with superpowers, and thankfully in recent years their stories are being told at length on the big screen too). But it does give a shorthand, rather than requiring me to spell out, and you to read, 'former Presidents and Prime Ministers' each time; it does give a sense of these women and men as a cohort, a group, with certain common characteristics; and it does convey the sense of specialness which attaches to them. Of course, other people are special, too: some former Deputy Prime Ministers, or Foreign Ministers, share many of the same skills and characteristics. Often, they hang around in the same forums, do the same jobs. Some of them, no doubt, are even more gifted. I don't disagree. And you'll meet some of them as you read this book. But this isn't a book about anyone who's ever held high public office. It's about the Ex Men and, like any other book about politics, it's ultimately about power. It's about how a particular group of people we thought had lost it haven't. And it's about what they choose to do with that power in their third career.

CHAPTER 1

HISTORY

It's a cold February day in London in early 2016, but inside the British Parliament the heating has been cranked right up and it's stifling. I'm sitting on an ornate but not enormously comfortable chair in the Queen's Robing Room, at one end of the Palace of Westminster. This means I'm surrounded by the shimmering gilts and opulent reds which are used as a not-so-subtle signifier that this is part of the House of Lords, the upper house of Parliament, and a far cry from the drab browns and greens of the House of Commons at the other end of the building. Like much else in this place, and some of the elderly politicians sitting around me, this distinction is a relic of a bygone era. But today this room is the setting for a remarkable story about how one man has attempted to make a horrible disease a relic of a bygone era. I, together with the ex-pols and some journalists hoping for a story about the upcoming presidential election, are waiting to hear from perhaps the most influential Ex Man of all: former US President Jimmy Carter. Carter is here to talk about one of his signature achievements, and as he is escorted in, he is greeted with a wave of applause and a swell of flashes from the scores of mobile phone cameras pointed in his direction. Those ex-pols may be Lords and Ladies these days, but they still recognise a real political superstar when they see one, even if they haven't been following his activities since leaving the White House terribly closely.

I, however, have been. I've been reading his books, keeping an eye on press cuttings and visited his presidential library in Atlanta, Georgia, but I haven't seen him in the flesh for eighteen years. Back then, I was a graduate student in the US and he was at a local bookshop signing copies of his book *The Virtues of Aging*. Today, it looks as though the lessons distilled in that book have borne rich fruit. For a 91-year-old man with a hectic schedule, he is in remarkably good condition. As the applause gives way to introductory remarks from Lord Chidgey, who has invited him here to speak about one of the most overlooked, least glamorous parts of the international healthcare scene, and a personal obsession of the former President for more than thirty years, Carter sits down and his eager eyes dart around the room. They twinkle as he smiles; and the room smiles back.

There's good reason for that. Carter is here to talk about neglected tropical diseases, which aren't present in wealthy countries and so drug companies have little incentive to study them or develop treatments. In other words, the diseases are neglected, explains Carter, because the people who live with them are neglected. But these people are just as intelligent and hard-working as us, he continues, and with family values which are just as good as ours. Jimmy Carter in 2016 doesn't sound all that different from Jimmy Carter in 1976, the year he ran for, and won, the presidency. The same Georgia accent, the same colloquial style, while politically his strong Christian faith, optimism and belief in universal human rights underpin his approach now just as they did then. And they did in 1986, too, when he decided that one focus of his post-presidential years would be eradicating guinea worm disease.

The story of how this happened is complicated, but it involves technological innovation, political progress and hard, sustained effort, all of it driven by Carter. He assembled experts who had recently vanquished smallpox, the only infectious disease ever to be eradicated from the earth; he asked corporate America for help creating a fibre which would prevent the spread of the disease; he worked with drug companies to develop ways of reducing the agonising emergence cycle for the worm; and he persuaded political and sometimes military leaders in Africa that it was possible to rid their people of this awful scourge, and that they should trust him to do it.

And now he's here, and the audience loves it. Now into his tenth decade, Carter has scaled back his public appearances and so this is a rare opportunity to see him up close and personal. He tells his audience a story about meeting one young woman in a village in Ghana who appeared to be holding a baby in her right arm. When he approached her, he discovered that it was actually her grossly swollen breast, with a guinea worm emerging from the nipple. She and others brought to meet him were clearly in agony. He hardly needs to make the point that aside from the human misery this infection was causing, people suffering in this way are often unable to work, to walk, to contribute to their families. Carter continues, describing the cycle of the guinea worm disease, a parasitic infection where over the course of a year the worm grows inside the body and then gradually makes its way out through a blister in the skin. The latter process, which can take thirty days, is agonising, and while very little can be done to shorten it, plunging it in water can ease the pain temporarily. And therein lies both the problem and the solution. The problem is that this infection is water-borne, so the plunging re-infects the water, spreads the disease and perpetuates the cycle. However, if the cycle can be interrupted, the worm will gradually die out – completely. As Carter tells it, the question confronting him in 1986 was how to interrupt the cycle.

For anyone who's read what he's written about guinea worm disease, this all sounds quite familiar. Like any good politician after months or years on the campaign trail, by now his stump speech contains the same stories, honed for maximum impact. But also like any good politician's stump speech, that doesn't make the details any less impressive. The goal of interrupting the cycle of the guinea worm once seemed unimaginably ambitious. In 1986, the year he decided to focus on it, there were an estimated 3.5 million infections worldwide, in at least twenty-one countries spanning Asia and Africa. The larvae were endemic in tens of thousands of villages, in some of the least hospitable and most dangerous places on earth. Yet working with health experts, pharmaceutical companies, a variety of political leaders and thousands of staff across the world, Carter has almost achieved it. By using specially developed materials to filter the larvae from drinking water, and educating millions of people about how to use them, the disease gradually receded. As it did, he and his people were able to focus ever more effort on the hold-out spots. By the end of 2019, the number of infections had fallen to just fifty-four. In the whole world. It's a stunning achievement, and even more so when the total cost is put into the equation: just $250 million over more than thirty years.

Of course, it's perfectly possible that someone else, an individual, an NGO, or perhaps a government, might have done this. Except no one did. And it is hard to imagine anyone else having the connections to reach the chairman of DuPont Chemicals, who offered to see if the company's scientists could develop a new non-rotting fibre to filter the water (they could); the President of Pakistan, General

Zia, to familiarise him with a problem endemic in his country; and Sudanese revolutionary rebel leader John Garang, to persuade him of the need for a ceasefire to get access to remote communities in his country. And Carter didn't stop there, tasking his centre to eliminate a series of other neglected tropical diseases which cause untold misery in some of the world's poorest countries: river blindness, lymphatic filariasis, schistosomiasis and trachoma.

This work would be enough for most people, but for the hyperactive, insatiable Carter, tackling tropical diseases has been just one of his post-presidential activities. And in each of them the secret ingredient, the singular strategy to Carter's success after leaving the White House, has been the web of relationships he has built, the consistency of his advocacy at every stage of his life and career, and how they all pull together. Presidential historian Douglas Brinkley called his book about Carter's time after office *The Unfinished Presidency* – with good reason. In the book, Brinkley notes Carter's symbiotic relationship with CNN, headquartered in Georgia. Carter would take CNN with him on trips – providing an immediate, global audience for his post-presidential activities while providing CNN with great access to breaking news stories about one of the world's most recognisable public figures.[1] The relationships Carter built in Latin America, and the respectful way he treated countries in his own hemisphere while he was in the White House, gave him a moral authority when talking about them after office. His work on farming productivity gave him an entrée with many African leaders anxious to expand their domestic production. Then, while he was there, he'd often talk about democracy, perhaps getting himself invited for an election-monitoring mission.

One of the constants is human rights. In the White House, Carter made human rights a centrepiece of his administration's foreign policy. He talked about it frequently, signed up to international agreements and gave Patt Derian, a civil and human rights activist whom he appointed to a beefed-up human rights job in the State Department, wide latitude in how she pursued the agenda. When fellow heads of government met Carter, they could expect human rights to be on the agenda, according to Curt Goering, who spent more than thirty years at Amnesty International and today is the executive director of the Center for the Victims of Torture. Carter's deep and personal commitment to human rights, says Goering, gave him a moral authority when it came to speaking about it after office. Which isn't to say that Carter was perfect: 'It was easier to go after countries where the risks of alienation were less, or in his calculus he could afford to do that; whereas the Middle East, for example, was probably a harder sell,' says Goering, acknowledging the trade-offs Carter made as President. 'But he made fewer of those and his consistency was far more than successors.'

What I find really interesting about Carter's human rights advocacy isn't so much his work on policy, though, because that is a President's job. Like any other political issue, you can advance it hard, or not so hard, or not at all. No, what made Carter different is what else he did in meetings with foreign heads of state. 'Amnesty would submit lists of prisoners, in the Philippines or in Argentina, people who we had information that they were picked up and then disappeared,' Goering tells me when we speak by phone. 'And sometimes Carter himself would raise the case, and sometimes it would be others in the administration.' Throughout his presidency, in scores of meetings with foreign heads of state, Carter would ask for the release of individual prisoners of conscience, and he carried on after leaving the White House. Before he asked a foreign leader, Carter needed to make very sure of the ground he was on. 'I remember for example conversations with Carter about individuals he had questions about, and is he on solid ground asking for the unconditional release of this particular person,' recalls Goering.

> Because if there's a criminal charge – that is, a recognisable crim-
> inal charge – you don't want to be asking one head of state to be
> asking another head of state for the release of someone uncondi-
> tionally if there's a question, maybe there's legitimate reasons to
> be holding this person. So we were always pretty careful to distin-
> guish – was this what we would call a prisoner of conscience, or
> was this a case where we needed further information before such
> a determination could be made?

Amnesty, at the time the pre-eminent human rights organisation, became an essential partner in this effort; the fact that the organi-sation won the Nobel Peace Prize in 1977 can't have done any harm either. And the relationship continued after Carter left office. Before travelling overseas, he would regularly be briefed on the people whose immediate and unconditional release he should request. In his post-presidential years, this was always done quietly, away from the cameras. And it worked. Brinkley, in his book on Carter published in 1998, reports that as many as 50,000 individuals could trace their release to Carter's requests; in the decades since, that number has grown substantially.

At various times since leaving office, Carter has intervened not just on behalf of human rights but on behalf of peace. Sometimes this has been with the support – tacit or public – of the sitting President; at other times, he has freelanced. In international hotspots as diverse as North Korea, Haiti, Sudan, Bosnia and the Middle East, Carter has interceded on behalf of what he sees as just and equitable solutions to intractable problems. And for all this work, Carter was rewarded in early October 2002 with his own Nobel Peace Prize, for what the Nobel Committee called 'his decades of untiring effort to find peaceful solutions to international conflicts, to advance democracy and human rights, and to promote economic and social development'. The timing was far from coincidental. In the aftermath of the 9/11 terrorist attacks against the United States, the Bush administration was pressing for action against Iraq and in early November the United Nations Security Council passed Resolution 1441, requiring Iraq to comply with weapons inspections and to disarm. Yet when he stood before the King of Norway and the other great and good gathered in Oslo in early December, Carter wanted to talk about peace. 'War may sometimes be a necessary evil,' he told them. 'But no matter how necessary, it is always an evil, never a good. We will not learn how to live together in peace by killing each other's children.' Appropriate enough, you might think – this ceremony was about receiving a peace prize, after all. But the convention is that former American Presidents don't criticise their successors' foreign policy in public, certainly not overseas, and never at times of heightened international tension. Carter, though, had never really bought into that convention, and has at times been harshly criticised for his politicking, even his meddling. In their fascinating book *The Presidents Club*, Nancy Gibbs and Michael Duffy give a real sense of the frustration, even fury, that every one of his successors has felt at times as Carter steadfastly refused to follow that protocol in one after another of those trouble spots on his hitlist. One of Bill Clinton's (unnamed) Cabinet members is quoted calling Carter a 'treasonous prick'.[2] At various points, that sentiment has surely been widely shared across both sides of the political aisle. But for all that, Carter is also much admired for his work, and sometimes much admired by people who are pretty hard-nosed about how the world works.

• • •

Three years after Carter spoke at the House of Lords, it's a sticky summer's evening and I'm sitting in a much more comfortable chair, in an office just the other side of Parliament Square. Westminster is seething with political intrigue as the latest showdown over Brexit looms. But I'm here to ask Steve Norris, a former Conservative Member of Parliament and minister who, as his Twitter biography has it, 'used to be the next Mayor of London', about something far removed from both. And so I switch the tape recorder on, take a sip of water and settle in as Norris tells me the story of the time he went to Panama with Jimmy Carter.

'The decision to actually call the election was taken by Noriega himself, under pressure from the Americans, but nonetheless he clearly called it,' Norris begins, explaining the complicated relationship between Panamanian strongman Manuel Noriega and the newly installed Bush administration in the United States.

> Everyone knew that Noriega was not a democrat. Noriega had simply taken control of the military and installed himself. But he kept onside with the Americans by effectively grassing up a few of his mates who were big in the drugs trade. And it was drugs that the US was primarily interested in stopping. They had, however, come to believe – as turned out to be the case – that Noriega was playing both sides against the middle, and he was hugely big in the narco trade himself, and he had to go.

It was in this political climate that Norris, with Carter and former US President Gerald Ford, together with a host of other current and former politicians from around the world, landed in Panama in May 1989 to monitor the elections. As Norris tells it, he and the other pols and ex-pols (including Ford) were very much part of the supporting cast, with Carter in the starring role.

> A team of us gathered from the four corners of the world. We were joined for a while by Gerald Ford, so we had both a Republican and a Democrat former President, but it was pretty obvious that he was there to play a bit of golf, and he never really took much of an active part in the whole process. Carter, on the other hand, was dedicated to the job in hand.

When Jimmy Carter started monitoring elections – and Panama was one of his first missions – it wasn't the standard fare it has since become. Election monitoring was in its early days, and for many of those involved having an energetic former American President on board gave a huge boost to their credibility, not to mention access to the key players and the media. But for all that, Carter didn't always make it simple. Sometimes, Norris tells me, 'his absolute sincerity and clarity and Christian conviction would lead him one way; those of us with a slightly more cynical disposition might have gone the other'. One of these disagreements arose when, just days before the election, Carter agreed to meet Noriega personally. Norris remembers warning Carter not to do it, as did everyone else. The concern, presumably, was that this meeting would give Noriega credibility?

> Yes, totally. Those are exactly the thoughts. That's why the CIA and the State Department and everybody else said, 'Don't do this, Jimmy, this is giving him an advantage which he will ruthlessly exploit.' And he did: every single paper in Panama the next day

had the picture on the front page. And it was all about 'mi amigo Jimmy', you know.

When the day of the election finally came, Norris was despatched to a small village north of the canal to watch the voting taking place. As a Spanish speaker, he was able to understand better than some of his fellow observers what was going on, and after meeting the man in charge and a few voters, was content with what he found. But that contentment didn't last.

> Their technique wasn't to do anything too obvious. One of them we stumbled across by accident. When I was in the village, a lorry turned up with a lot of young soldiers in it, and soldiers had a particular voting privilege. Because they were allegedly on active service, they were able to vote wherever they happened to be on the day, so they went in and showed their pass, and then they could vote. And so they all did.

Norris decided he had seen all he could see in the first village, and so set off for the second. 'It wasn't long before our car could see in the distance the army truck, and exactly what I think you can imagine did transpire.' Sure enough, there were the soldiers, voting again.

> I didn't want to go to a third, in case the car 'had an accident'. But it was obvious what was happening, and by the time I got back, which was late night on polling day, the kinds of stories which were coming out from all my colleagues were more or less the same as mine. The election was not open and it was not honest.

'What then happened', Norris continues, 'was the extraordinary story of Carter's personal bravery when we were attempting to enter the counting centre. And this was where he saw an officer, in officer's uniform, carrying a ballot box out of the centre.' Standing nearby, Norris was close enough to see and hear the ensuing conversation.

He stopped him and in English said, 'Where are you going with that?', and the man mumbled something or other, clearly not to Carter's content. And he uttered this line which I've never forgotten: 'Are you a thief or are you an honest man?' And he looked the guy right in the eye. And the guy you could see sort of thinking, 'Oh fuck,' but to his credit the guy turned around, went back in, and probably said, 'Lose this one round the back.'

Norris likes to tell a tale, and he tells this one well, but he wants me to know that this was genuinely dangerous. When the election monitors packed up for the night and left the counting centre for their hotel, a mob had formed; by the time they tried to return, the situation was so combustible that Carter's protection detail advised the rest of the observers that they could protect only him. 'I'm not given to massive exaggeration – I mean, being in politics I must exaggerate somewhat. But you're in a fairly tense situation. It's not like Epping Forest elections,' says Norris, referring to his former constituency just outside London.

That was typical Carter. This was very dangerous. We knew this election had been thrown, and it was very obvious that Noriega was going to win, and we weren't going to stop him, and we were going to write a report saying the election was thrown and he didn't give a shit. But Carter nonetheless put himself on the line.

I think Norris is worth hearing on Carter because he's not particularly sympathetic politically. But up close he's seen much to admire. Which is perhaps why, the following February, he found himself back in Central America with the former US President, this time in Nicaragua. Here, the politics were more straightforward.

The background to this is that the US under Reagan and later under George Bush Sr was financing the Contras, who were fighting in turn against the Sandinista regime, which was a very left-wing, allegedly popular group, led by the Ortega brothers, which in resisting the Contras had produced a very unhappy situation in an already very unhappy country.

Managua, the capital city, was still suffering the effects of a massive earthquake almost twenty years earlier, leaving many buildings uninhabitable and very poor housing conditions. But not all suffering was equal. 'Behind very neutral walls lived some very wealthy people, most of whom had put their money into Miami,' Norris continues.

This was the sort of situation you saw – wealth in the hands of the few, a government which was ostensibly a government for the people but which had become increasingly unpopular as young mothers saw their sons murdered by the Contras. And that's exactly what the US in its wisdom wanted to deliver because they were paranoid about communism and socialism and anything that smacked of left-wingery.

Inside Nicaragua, elections had been called and the Sandinistas faced a challenge from the National Opposition Union (UNO) a united front of opposition forces – Norris says it was clear they were funded by money from behind those anonymous adobe walls. Norris was again sent out of the capital to observe the election; only this time he didn't find any nasty surprises. 'The election itself took place under conditions which were remarkably honest,' says Norris. 'From what I could see, the voting process was perfectly relaxed, people were able to vote.' There was one slight hiccup, though. 'When it came to the counting, I found myself acting returning of-ficer, because the official had clearly never supervised an election before,' Norris remembers with a smile. 'So, with perfect goodwill on their side, I was the one who would take out each ballot paper, show it and then allocate it to the pile, so they could see it was being done entirely honestly.' As he did, the likely result of the election became increasingly obvious: 'It was clear there that the UNO coa-lition had won.'

But if the actual result was obvious, how the government would receive that news was not.

When the news was communicated to Ortega that he'd lost, it was obvious that he and his brother and many of the people around him really were tempted at least to say, 'You know what, this is just all that dirty money from Miami and the Americans, why don't we just throw the whole thing?' And this is where Carter comes into his own.

Carter already knew Daniel Ortega; Ortega knew he didn't represent the pro-Contra faction currently in the White House, and he knew and understood that when Carter tried to persuade him that con-ceding the election was the right thing to do, it was more than just empty rhetoric. Back in the capital the following morning, Norris and the other observers regrouped. The situation was tense, with police and military people loyal to Ortega all around. But Carter had been busy and was again apparently oblivious to the risks. 'It was clear that Carter had spent virtually the whole of the night with the Ortega brothers, convincing them – or at least proselytising very heavily – that they should respect the result,' remembers Norris. And it worked: waiting at the Olof Palme Convention Centre in the centre of Managua, where the counting was taking place, Norris and the other observers watched as Ortega conceded the election.

But Carter's diplomacy wasn't confined to Managua – or Panama City. After watching Noriega throw the election in Panama, Carter flew back to Washington DC and reported back to the Bush administration. By the end of the year, after mounting tensions between the countries, Bush authorised the invasion of Panama and the arrest of Noriega. He was captured and flown to the US, where he was prosecuted, convicted and ultimately spent seventeen years in prison. Carter's reaction to the Nicaraguan episode produced a very different result. Historian Iwan Morgan, who calls Carter a 'foreign policy entrepreneur', notes that he 'persuaded Bush and Secretary of State James Baker to agree a deal whereby the US-backed Contra rebels were disbanded but the Sandinistas kept control of the army'.[3]

There is a coda. Daniel Ortega ran repeatedly to recover his office, and was eventually re-elected President in 2006, and he's still in power now. Norris today is sceptical about the governance of Nicaragua – whether it's by Ortega, the UNO coalition or their successors. But he's also in no doubt about the value of the change of government in 1990, in which Jimmy Carter played the central role. 'Nicaragua's in a better place than it would have been,' he tells me, unambiguously. Carter has monitored dozens of election missions across the world since 1990, but these two early missions showed good Jimmy and bad Jimmy. On the one hand, the power of personal connection, an overwhelming belief in democracy and human rights, and a moral and physical courage in speaking up for those beliefs; on the other, the arrogance and need to be in charge which has been reported by many who worked with Carter over the years. Strikingly, in the final part of his post-presidential career, these traits were almost completely absent.

• • •

It's easy to forget now, after years of post-presidential activism, that when he left office in 1981 Jimmy Carter was regarded as a failure, even a joke. For all the policies, personal connections and human decency which gave him a platform for his post-presidency, and for all the decisions he took which in hindsight look foresighted, as President he often failed to deal with the most pressing concerns of the American people. Many Americans remember sky-high inflation, the oil crisis, a speech which seemed to say America couldn't solve its problems, and a failed hostage rescue. The beige cardigan he wore for another presidential address seemed, somehow, to sum up his administration. Meanwhile, political insiders still tell stories about his legendary micro-managing, with Carter going so far as to approve bookings on the White House tennis court. Of course, some of this was simple bad luck, but the know-all arrogance that Steve Norris saw in Panama before the meeting with Noriega was also part of the problem. The result was noxious for Carter's reputation. He became a punchline for his successors, and even his fellow Democrat Bill Clinton, elected fully twelve years after Carter left office, kept his distance. And so Carter's reputational rehabilitation took a long time. Battling infectious diseases, making peace and winning that Nobel Prize certainly helped. But amid the many other causes Carter has championed in the four decades since he left office, one above all has helped transform the way Americans, in particular, view their former President.

'He said, "What I'd like to know, President and Mrs Carter, is if you would be interested and would you consider coming to work on a construction site, and actually help us build a house, some-time?", and then he posed the question, "Are you interested, or are you very interested?"' Civil rights activist Linda Fuller is describing the moment her husband asked Jimmy Carter to support the small housing NGO they had founded together, Habitat for Humanity. 'They kind of chuckled and looked at each other. I can remember that moment in my head so clearly.' She pauses as she remembers Carter's response. 'Well, I suppose we're very interested,' replied the former President. But Carter is nothing if not a practical man, so he asked the Fullers to think a little and write up a list of specific ways he could be helpful. A couple of weeks later, after working hard to boil down the list to fifteen items, Linda and Millard Fuller were back again in the former President and First Lady's living room. 'We went through, item by item. I think [Millard] had listed: help us fundraise, get very involved not only in constructing houses here in Americus but in other areas that we were working around the country and around the world,' Linda Fuller remembers. 'But when we got through the list, Millard said, "Well, which ones appeal to you? Which ones do you think you'd like to do?" And they said, "All of them!"' I'm speaking to her down the phone from her home in Georgia, but close to forty years later, as she laughs and repeats, 'All of them', I can hear the amazement in her voice. 'We just were higher than a kite.'

The relationship matured gradually, and in time Carter would lend his name to Habitat for Humanity, bring his friends on board and raise millions of dollars for them. But, like his work with Amnesty on prisoners of conscience, Carter didn't feel he was above supporting one person at a time. In the autumn of 1984 came what the current chief executive of Habitat for Humanity, Jonathan Reckford, calls the organisation's 'coming-out party'. The two couples, the Carters and the Fullers, scooped up a group of friends, chartered a Greyhound bus and headed to New York City to work on a Habitat project. Habitat for Humanity builds housing for people with low incomes, who receive help building their homes and zero-interest loans but must put in what Fuller calls 'sweat equity' – they have to work on the houses themselves. The project in New York City was enormous – a six-storey building containing twenty apartments – and the former President and Mrs Carter arrived each morning and worked long shifts alongside all the other volunteers. The *New York Times* reported that the former President had to leave the site mid-afternoon on the first day for a brief press conference, but otherwise knuckled down. 'It's O.K. if they want to take my picture holding a hammer,' it quotes him saying, 'but as long as I'm holding a hammer, it's going to be hitting a nail.'⁴ Habitat for Humanity reaped the benefits. 'It hit the press big time, as you can imagine. Our growth was pretty significant up to that point. But when they ran that first Jimmy Carter work project, the graph that we made showed the tracking going straight up,' Linda Fuller remembers.

I mean from then on, we had phenomenal growth. They have done more than thirty Jimmy Carter work projects now. They're both in their nineties, they're limited a little bit in what they can do, but President Carter's a worker. He doesn't let a minute go by that he's not actively working on something.

Today, in her seventies herself, Fuller still sounds astonished when she looks back on Carter's commitment. 'They were so busy with their own work, but they always honoured their commitment to give a week of their time every year.'

Reckford, who has run the organisation now for fifteen years and been on work projects with Carter on several continents, agrees. 'I've been with him with Presidents of countries and heads of state, and I've been with him with some of the poorest people in world, and he's always the same person,' he says. 'And that could be frustrating to people, but I think it's an incredible mark of integrity.' And, like Linda Fuller, he's clear about the impact Carter has had on the organisation. 'I don't think you're able to overstate the impact they've had on opening the doors and being role models for what community volunteerism can look like.' At the 2019 project in Nashville, Tennessee, Carter slipped and fell and cut his head on the day of the build. But he still showed up – with a big bandage, and a huge bruise covering his eye and cheek. 'The image of a 95-year-old ex-President getting stitches and then coming out to the build site, I mean he enjoyed that, but it's just such an example of that Depression-era intense work ethic and commitment to everything he gets involved with,' says Reckford. That picture went around the world and garnered Habitat three times as much press as normal, and he tells me that builds with Carter involved can attract ten times as many volunteers, too. Many want to work on the Carter house, particularly the VIPs, and Reckford laughs as he tells me how he tries to warn them that it will be extra hard work. 'We always joke: it's not a competition as long as President Carter's house gets done first.'

Habitat has built homes in dozens of countries since it began, and Carter has been on a number of them. After we speak, Reckford sends me photos of Carter over the years: here he is with the other

volunteers in New York City in 1984; here rendering the front of a
home in Mexico in 1986; here handing over the keys to a young girl
in the Philippines in 1999; here measuring some plywood in Texas
in 2014. But the story he tells me is of the Philippines, which he
heard from another volunteer and which has entered Habitat folklore. 'It was incredibly hot,' he begins.

> At that point they were on an incredibly strict schedule because
> if you didn't get each day's work done, you wouldn't stay on track.
> So people had been working all day long, it was about six o'clock,
> they were exhausted, they were getting on the buses. President
> Carter was walking around asking people to get back off the bus
> so they would hit their mark for the day. And he walks by, inspect-
> ing each house, and he tells the house manager, 'I see you haven't
> got your toilet in, you really need to get your toilet in tonight, and
> your son next door hasn't got his in either. If I show you how to
> put it in, will you show your son how to put his in?' And so what
> do you say, other than, 'Of course'? And at seven o'clock at night,
> in ninety degrees, President Carter is in this tiny space teaching
> him how to put in the cement, seal and lay and balance a toilet.

He pauses, incredulity in his voice. 'Can you imagine any other
head of state doing that?'

It wasn't just one-way traffic, though. While Habitat for Humanity was registering the volunteers, building the homes, cashing the
cheques and having its message about affordable housing amplified
the world over, Carter also reaped the benefits of the association.
In fact, it was essential to his public rehabilitation. Those pictures
of the former President putting his carpentry skills to use on a
building site for low-income Americans helped centre his decency

and diligence in the public mind. And when I ask her whether they knew it would be good for his image, as well as for Habitat, Linda Fuller is in no doubt.

> Oh yes, we were, and that was OK … I think that they did enjoy the notoriety that came from their work with Habitat for Humanity. In fact, since they did send out a lot of letters asking people to get involved with Habitat for Humanity, I suppose the largest percentage of the supporters thought he started Habitat for Humanity. And Millard said, 'Well, that's OK. It doesn't matter who gets the credit!'

Less welcome was the price to be paid for this reputational rehabilitation. And it's a price which, according to both Jonathan Reckford and Linda Fuller, Carter still rails against. 'President Carter hated it when people said, "Well, he wasn't such a good President but he sure is a great ex-President,"' she tells me.

> He hated that because in his mind, he was a good President. He took that job very seriously, but any President runs up against so much opposition that there was so much more he wanted to do than he was able to do under the high pressures that are in Washington. He thought he did a pretty good job, and I do too.

• • •

When Carter left office, he joined a club with only two other members: former US Presidents Richard Nixon and Gerald Ford. Ford was never much interested in Carter's kind of activism, and it wasn't an option for Nixon, still under a cloud after his impeachment.

There weren't many contemporary examples Carter could look to overseas, either: in 1981, a relatively small proportion of the world's countries were democracies; of those which were, most former leaders were elderly and tended not to do much of note after leaving office. Even had they wanted to, there weren't many opportunities: only the European Commission, the civil service of what is now the European Union, provided any kind of second (or third) career.[5] The result was that most former Presidents and Prime Ministers either remained in politics or retired altogether. But Carter did have one predecessor he could look to for a possible model. And although Carter might not appreciate the comparison, there are some startling similarities between him and Herbert Hoover. Like Carter, Hoover was a single-term President. Like Carter, despite a stellar career both as an engineer and as a politician before winning the White House, Hoover's presidency was widely regarded as a failure. Like Carter, Hoover's methodical approach, prodigious determination to do good, religious motivation and phenomenal work ethic meant that by the time of his death, more than thirty years after leaving office, his reputation had been restored. And like Carter, he really had to fight for redemption the hard way. Hoover lost his battle for re-election in 1932 in a landslide. For years, no political candidate wanted to be seen with Hoover; he was exiled from political life, and Franklin Roosevelt, the man who beat him, seemed to go out of his way to humiliate the former President. Hoover seethed, but he kept active with various charitable endeavours, in 1936 taking on a role as chairman of the Boys Club of America. But still he waited…

In the end, he had to wait twelve years – indeed, until Roosevelt died – even to be invited back to the White House. When he was, the relationship he formed with the new President, Harry Truman, was to change the lives of millions of people across the world. Most immediately, there was the task of feeding hundreds of millions of people. It's little remembered now, largely because most didn't starve, but immediately after the Second World War crops failed across the world and millions of people did not have enough food to eat. Hoover had made his name in just such a dire situation after the First World War, organising a vast relief effort which both saved food and moved it to where it needed to be, saving millions of lives and earning him the moniker 'The Great Humanitarian'. Now Truman asked the 71-year-old former President to revisit his greatest triumph; Hoover agreed, and undertook a gruelling, months-long tour of thirty-eight countries to ascertain the scale of the problem. He recommended dramatic, sustained action, and as well as reporting back to Truman, who largely accepted his recommendations, he took his case to the American public, to persuade them of the need to sacrifice a little of their food so that other families, thousands of miles away, might also be fed. For the second time in thirty years, Hoover's work helped save millions of lives. By now, the conservative Republican Hoover and liberal Democrat Truman, running for election as President in his own right, had become unlikely confidants – friends, even. But when Truman asked the former President to chair a commission to reorganise the US federal government, even a friend might have baulked. Hoover thought otherwise, ultimately chairing two commissions which recommended a wholesale reorganisation of the executive branch, from the national security state to scientific research and health and education.

• • •

There's a brief pause on the other end of the phone when I ask whether he regrets retiring from politics, and then, 'No, I don't think so. I've done a lot of interesting things since. I'm always more interested in what happens next week,' he adds. In the case of Malcolm Fraser, a former Prime Minister of Australia, that is an understatement. Fraser was just fifty-two when he left office in 1983, even younger than Jimmy Carter, and his search for productive ways to contribute did indeed lead him to do some very interesting things. But while they overlap with Carter, they're also different, and round out the types of activities that Ex Men get up to, and which this book is about.

That line – 'I'm always more interested in what happens next week' – just about sums up Fraser's life as an Ex Man: a restless, ambitious character. I'm speaking to him just after he's published his memoirs – twenty-seven years after leaving office, and with historian Margaret Simons as co-author because he wanted, as she describes it, 'to expose his record to a questioning if not a critical eye … He wanted to be questioned.'[6] The book helps explain how Fraser, who in office was a polarising figure of the right – a Thatcherite before Thatcher, who came to office in highly controversial circumstances – in his eighties has become a darling of the liberal left. It is, he explains to me on the phone, about values.

> People forget there are different sorts of loyalties. And different loyalties – all of which are valid in their own right – can conflict very seriously. You can have a loyalty to friends, but how far does that go if your friend transgresses in very serious ways? You can have a loyalty to party, but how far do you have to carry that if you find the party violating values which you believe are enormously important for a civilised society? Or you can have a loyalty to values which you believe either should govern behaviour or which create some kind of standard by which you want to live.

There's a pause, 'Erm…', and a breath, 'and I'm afraid I was one of those who gave greater weight to loyalty to values as I believe them to be'. That's putting it mildly. In the book they co-authored, Margaret Simons writes that, at the age of fifty-two, Fraser wasn't ready to retire.

> He soon discovered that Australia doesn't know what to do with former prime ministers who still have energy and talent to offer. Corporations didn't want him. He made a few abortive ventures in consultancy, only to pull back when it became clear that companies wanted not his advice but for him to use his contacts and connections on their behalf. Fraser felt this was an improper use of his former position.[7]

And so, Fraser funnelled much of his energy into projects – often overseas – which fitted his values. These involved working to end apartheid in South Africa; joining with a number of friends and colleagues to form the InterAction Council, a club for Ex Men; running the major humanitarian charity CARE; and ultimately, just months before leaving the party he had once led, helping persuade his successor to join his nation's apology to aboriginal Australians over the scandal of the 'stolen generations'.

South Africa was arguably the most significant of these. Fraser did two important jobs, first chairing a United Nations committee on the role of transnational companies in South Africa during the apartheid era, and then co-chairing a Commonwealth Eminent Persons Group trying to find a way to bring that era to an end. The first job opened his eyes to the horrors of apartheid, the overarching legal framework that kept different racial groups in South Africa separated, with whites in charge of public life and black South

Africans not only disenfranchised but subjected to coercive control in almost every aspect of their daily lives. The second job was an opportunity to do something about this evil system. For several months, and in three separate visits to South Africa and the wider southern African region in the spring of 1986, Fraser and his co-chair, Olusegun Obasanjo, a former Nigerian head of state whom he had got to know while Prime Minister, talked to every group in South Africa. They devised a 'superglue' rule during these visits – that no matter how seriously they were provoked, they would not get up and leave; instead, they would stay glued to their seats and keep talking, because ultimately that was the only way a solution could be found.[8] To do so, they had to navigate serious distrust on all sides. The Eminent Persons Group had been established in the first place to paper over a schism within the Commonwealth between UK Prime Minister Margaret Thatcher on one side, who believed in constructive engagement with South Africa, and most Commonwealth countries on the other, who wanted sanctions on the racist South African regime. Once established, Fraser and Obasanjo had to build enough trust so that both the South African government and the principal opposition party – the outlawed African National Congress – would meet them. I asked Fraser whether his experience as a Prime Minister helped with this process. 'Well, I don't know whether that made it easier, but I could see where people might be going to go wrong,' he replies.

For example, the Commonwealth, when they agreed to establish this group, wrote out a one-page list of demands for the government of South Africa. And I just looked at it and said, 'All right, you send this off, we'll all pack up and go home. None of us will ever get to South Africa. We'll go there without conditions.' It took me three days to persuade Commonwealth officials. I think they might have thought it was beneath dignity to go there without conditions. Well, I knew the conditions they wanted accepted would result in us not getting anywhere. I mean, the ANC were looking on with some suspicion. Not only the government. We had to win trust. We had to set out a way of operating that would enable us to do our job, trying to find what needed to be done if genuine negotiations were going to take place.

In the end, while this strategy succeeded in getting them into the country, the South African government refused to engage constructively with the ANC. But the work that Fraser and Obasanjo did together, and the relationship they built, would have two important consequences for Africa. The first was the report they produced, 'Mission to South Africa', which provided an unvarnished account of the horrors of apartheid, from two serious and well-regarded former Ex Men (as well as the other members of the group, handpicked by various Commonwealth governments). It could not be lightly dismissed, and helped build the case for further action. As interesting was the second consequence – the role Fraser played in Obasanjo's life, and in Nigeria's politics. Obasanjo is a fascinating figure, and one whom Fraser much admired: a former military ruler who came to power in the mid-1970s following a coup but speedily set about transferring power back to civilian rule. Leaving politics behind, Obasanjo set up a farm, but he never lost his political ambitions – and in the mid-1990s those ambitions got him into trouble with Nigeria's military ruler, Sani Abacha, who had Obasanjo sentenced to life in prison.

More than a decade after my conversation with Fraser, I get the chance to ask Olusegun Obasanjo about the relationship between the two men. I've been told that Fraser, and the wider network of Ex Men, swung into action when he was jailed. 'What happened was that the InterAction Council, working individually and collectively, [former British Prime Minister] Jim Callaghan, [former West German Chancellor] Helmut Schmidt, [former Canadian Prime Minister] Pierre Trudeau, Malcolm Fraser, they on their own wrote to Abacha,' Obasanjo tells me. He has a deep, gravelly voice, and speaks slowly so that you are forced to pay attention to every word. 'Jim Callaghan called him on the telephone, I know that, got other people to call … The InterAction Council as a body, collectively and individually, was very, very helpful in mounting pressure on Abacha for my release.' It wasn't just the InterAction Council: Jimmy Carter also took a close interest, and together they got his sentence reduced to fifteen years, although it wasn't until Abacha's death in 1998 that he was freed. The next year, Obasanjo ran for and won the presidency, and was re-elected in 2003. His presidency embedded democracy in Nigeria (although all of the elected Presidents have been former generals, leading one commentator to wryly title a chapter about Nigerian post-presidential politics 'An army of ex-presidents').[9] And so the interventions on Obasanjo's behalf, including from Fraser and his colleagues on the InterAction Council, bent the arc of history in Africa's most populous nation, and its largest economy.

The second of Malcolm Fraser's major international contributions, and one of the ways in which he re-imagined the possible roles a former Prime Minister could fill, was in his relationship with the international development NGO CARE. Between its Australian branch, which he served as founding chairman, and CARE International, where he was President, Fraser was with the organisation for a total of fifteen years. He was deeply involved in every aspect of establishing CARE Australia, he travelled on its behalf overseas and, much like Jimmy Carter's work on guinea worm disease or with Habitat for Humanity, he opened doors wherever he went. In his book, he recalls entering a meeting with one of the warring factions in the Somali civil war. The heavily armed men stood up and said, 'Prime Minister! Welcome!'[10] Later that decade, he successfully negotiated with the Yugoslav regime of Slobodan Milošević for the release of three CARE employees who were being held by the country; again, as with Carter and his various missions, a combination of Fraser's ability as a negotiator and his status as a former Prime Minister carried the day.

But at home in Australia, Fraser's position as a former Prime Minister was changing. On issue after issue, but particularly on questions around identity and ethnicity, and who could and could not be considered an Australian, he found himself increasingly estranged from his party. As he spoke out, senior party members spoke out against him. The two sides were heading for a highly contentious divorce, but before the final breach Fraser had one final contribution to make to Australian public life. In 2008, the new Labor Prime Minister, Kevin Rudd, wanted to issue a formal apology to Australia's aboriginal communities for a decades-long policy under which many tens of thousands of mixed-race aboriginal children were taken from their families, homes and communities and raised in church or state institutions. It had been a decade since a government inquiry had established the full horror of what had happened, and Rudd was keen to begin the healing process. Fraser strongly supported the apology, and tried to convince the leader of his party, Brendan Nelson, to make it a bipartisan effort. 'I spoke to Nelson in particular, and I think I had some influence in making sure that he joined the apology,' he tells me, before adding quickly, 'although half of what he said was fine and half of what he said was really an apology to his right wing, who didn't want him to apologise.' He chuckles to himself. Bearing in mind the breakdown of his relationship with his party, this seems to me a good time to ask about private influence and public influence, and Fraser answers without hesitation.

> If you've got a good relationship with the person, doing it privately is better. But if you know a relationship for a particular reason has gone beyond a certain point, then all you can try and do really is – if you think the issue is important enough – to put your view on the public record.

• • •

Between them, Carter and Fraser took on and developed all the roles, all the different ways of being, that are available to the Ex Men. And over the next seven chapters, I'll say more about each of them.

But above all else, this book is about power, and influence, and the limits of both. It's a deeply nebulous subject of course, even for those in office, but when the levers are often intangible, influence can be really hard to discern. And beyond that, it's about how influence translates into change: are they making a difference? My starting point in writing this book is that if being in the room where decisions are made – and Ex Men often can gain access to that room – is sufficiently valuable that companies and individuals spend millions of pounds and thousands of hours trying to get there, it's worth doing – but it almost certainly isn't enough. The savvier Ex Men in this book, and those working with them, know this. For them, this question of effecting change is ever-present. Mabel van Oranje, who has worked with George Soros at the Open Society Foundations, with a number of Ex Men at The Elders, another of the members' clubs, and now with Nobel Peace Prize winner Malala Yousafzai, agrees that this is the key question to ask. One of the earliest initiatives of The Elders was on child marriage. We talk about it for almost an hour and a half, shooting over the time she set aside for the conversation. But when we come to the end, she asks for a couple more moments of my time to tell me this:

> The Elders really played a catalytic role [in putting child marriage on the global agenda], and I find it very hard to imagine how so much progress would have happened so quickly without them. Without The Elders there might still be zero progress. We might still not know about child marriage. Or maybe we would have, but not with programmes all over the world, and donor money going to it. You can't go anywhere nowadays without hearing about child marriage. Of course, that then gets me worried: everyone's talking about it, but what are they actually doing? More than thirty countries now have national strategies to end child marriage. How is that being implemented? What does it mean? Are child marriage rates actually going down?

It's a really frank admission of the limits of how much we can really know, and the importance of trying to find out. That's what the rest of this book is about: how the Ex Men are still changing the world.

CHAPTER 2

CLUBS

At a luxury hotel on the banks of the river Liffey just outside Dublin, it's a little after seven on a Friday evening in May 2019. It's been raining outside, and under the curious gaze of American tourists returning from a day on the hotel's immaculate golf courses, a stream of people in suits is gradually filling a reception room. At the drinks table inside, I get chatting to a former politician, and after introducing ourselves she tells me what to expect this weekend, what to look out for, who I'm likely to find most illuminating. She's generous with her time, charming and interesting, but I can't help being slightly distracted because over her shoulder I can see a former Prime Minister of Canada walk in. There's a former President of Switzerland. A former Prime Minister of Malta. A former Taoiseach of Ireland. Some of them come over to greet the minister, and she introduces me to them. A former Australian Foreign Minister wanders over and, upon hearing about this book, he tells me I ought to quote something he said a few years ago. I promise I'll look it up. As the room fills, I fall into conversation with a well-connected philanthropist, an investor, businessmen of various political shades and none. The room warms as it fills, and I find myself back beside the former minister. A few minutes later there is a slight stir, and there he is. The chairman wanders through the

assembled throng, welcoming people to his annual meeting, smil-
ing and glad-handing. He comes over to the former minister, they
greet each other warmly, and she introduces us. We've met before,
actually, but it was eleven years ago and there is no reason why F. W.
de Klerk, the Nobel Laureate and former President of South Africa,
the man who ended apartheid in South Africa, will remember me.
And so I say hello, thank him for his welcome and let him continue
on his way around the room. De Klerk isn't especially known for his
love of the limelight, including the media. 'It's liberating to be more
of a private citizen again,' he told me eleven years earlier, when I
asked him about losing the presidency, 'an interesting new liberty
to be your own man again. And I never regretted retiring.' Retiring
isn't a word most of us would use to describe what he does now; this
organisation is testimony to that. But it is conducted largely out of
the limelight, and this organisation of his, the Global Leadership
Foundation (GLF), whose annual meeting I've been invited to observe in action, is almost comically low-profile. I've spent the best
part of a decade trying to get in and see what goes on, and I've been
granted access, and permission to write about what happens here,
on Chatham House rules – that I don't reveal the details of who said
what. That's partly because of what they do and how they do it; but
it's also because de Klerk's personality and sensibilities run through
this organisation like lettering through the centre of a stick of rock.
The GLF gets a lot of its credibility and legitimacy from who he is,
and what he did, and how he operates. In return, this Ex Man and
the others he brings together get to do something meaningful and,
perhaps, important.

The best way to describe the organisation is as a club-consultancy.
The club members are for the most part, like the former minister,
old pals of de Klerk's. Certainly, in the early days there was a core

group of African Ex Men and those from Western countries with an established interest in Africa – people like former Botswanan President Ketumile Masire and former US Assistant Secretary of State for African Affairs Chester Crocker. These days it's more diverse, with Ex Men from every continent represented amongst the membership. This, their annual gathering, is a chance to get together, to catch up with old friends, talk shop, do a bit of business and perhaps reminisce about when they used to run the world. And around the room they're doing just that. When the drinks are over and we head to dinner, many of them pair off to continue their conversations. As I watch them, and make my own way through to the dining room, I'm reminded of a quote from another Ex Man, the former West German Chancellor Helmut Schmidt, about a similar gathering of Ex Men, that it was 'a conspiracy of former world leaders against present world leaders. But thank God none of us has the power to do anything anymore.'[1] And I wonder about every part of his quip.

Schmidt wasn't a member of this club, but he was a member of one of the others. Because F. W. de Klerk wasn't the first to gaze upon his fellow Ex Men and sense possibility. There's the Club of Madrid, The Elders, the InterAction Council and the GLF, as well as several regional organisations for African, Asian and Latin American Ex Men. They all speak the same kind of language, the kind of language you'll find throughout this book: of democracy, human rights, free markets and respect for the rule of law – the language of a globalised, liberal world order, in other words. On its website, the Club of Madrid, for example, says its mission is to 'support and foster democratic values ... to strengthen democratic leadership and institutional capacity ... to better tackle major global challenges'. And what are those challenges? The club currently runs three projects: a 'shared societies project', a 'preventing and countering violent extremism' project and a 'next-generation democracy' project. The Elders' mission, meanwhile, is to 'use our independence, collective experience and influence to work for peace, justice and human rights worldwide'. But just because this bland, corporate language is torpor-inducing, it doesn't mean that these clubs aren't intriguing. And two, in particular, stand out: the GLF and The Elders. There are a lot of similarities: each was founded by a former South African President, each initially funded by a wealthy benefactor, each bears the mark of their founders' and funders' personalities, and each is headquartered in central London – about a mile apart, as it happens. And the fact that these two former Presidents succeeded one another, and even for a time served together as President and Vice-President in the government of national unity, is certainly noteworthy. But what makes them really interesting is that each seems to know how their organisation fits into the globalised liberal world, and what, uniquely, it can do: in other words, they have a clear purpose. However, that is where the similarities don't so much end as grind to a screeching standstill. For while de Klerk's publicity-shy GLF operates quietly, behind the scenes, and is careful to preserve the privacy of what they do and how, The Elders, founded by Nelson Mandela and funded by the flamboyant British businessman Richard Branson, is much more media-friendly, often choosing public campaigning and open dialogue where the GLF chooses quiet discussion.

And over the course of my weekend with them, I watch as many of the GLF's funders and guests take their chances to speak to the Ex Men, whether it's to gather some pearls of wisdom, hear an old war story or perhaps to whisper quietly about some concern of their own. I do the same, and you'll read about some of what they tell me later in this book. But as we talk, it becomes clear that at the core of the GLF are the club members and their friendships. They huddle together over breakfast and in the coffee breaks and chat over lunch and dinner. As the organisers call each meeting to order, a few always wander in from the hallways a minute or two late, gossiping over cups of coffee. It's giving me a sense of déjà vu, because this isn't the first gathering of Ex Men I've been to, nor the first club.

• • •

Exactly four years earlier, at another luxury hotel, this time on the banks of the river Usk just outside Newport, in south Wales, it's just after nine on a Wednesday morning. As hotel guests head out for a morning of golf on the links, the assembled Ex Men are being introduced to a group of pupils from some local schools before taking part in a question-and-answer session with them. This is the annual meeting of the InterAction Council, the oldest club for Ex Men. As I watch the reasonably predictable questions and their reasonably predictable answers, I ponder how useful these sorts of events are, and what they achieve beyond the undeniable warm feelings, a few selfies and the sense of engaging with 'youth' they give the Ex Men. Perhaps that's just the cynical journalist in me – the students seem to appreciate these old men making an attempt to answer with humour and the occasional burst of candour. The colourful former Colombian President Andrés Pastrana is a particular hit, as he jumps in on a question about the effect of the drug trade in his country and emphasises, with some passion, the importance of young people getting involved in politics.

But then something surprising happens. One of the students asks a question about the fighting in Ukraine, which has been in the news for months on end. Viktor Zubkov, a former Russian Prime Minister and current chairman of Russian energy giant Gazprom, perma-tanned and permanently surrounded by beefy security men, gets up to answer. He thanks the student and welcomes the question but suggests that perhaps it is best answered privately, later, tomorrow. Surely his colleague from Ukraine will agree? As his colleague from Ukraine rises to his feet, he pauses for a moment to compose himself. He does agree: these issues must be discussed tomorrow. But Viktor Yushchenko, the country's former President and one-time leader of Ukraine's Orange Revolution, a man who bears the scars of that experience on his face, clearly doesn't feel that the assembled students should return home unenlightened about the threat Russia poses not just in the east of his country but around the world. In fact, in a diatribe which is remarkable for its almost total lack of diplomatic nicety, he proceeds to lay the blame for more or less everything that is wrong with the world, and certainly those things which had made it onto the InterAction Council's agenda for the next three days, at Russia's feet. If this is the opening salvo, it makes me wonder what tomorrow's session might bring, and looking around I sense the same calculation on the faces of several Ex Men.

Anyway, that's the end of the opening ceremony, and the Ex Men head off for lunch. It is a good and generous lunch and during the session immediately afterwards, entitled 'The Present State of the World', that goodness and generosity does perhaps diminish the level of engagement. I watch as one participant dozes off, another kicks off his shoes, a third is chewing his false teeth. Several make long and what I think might charitably be described as 'performative' contributions as the volunteer staff jot down the salient points, from which they will later extract some wisdom with which to mould the end-of-council communiqué. But that's still a couple of days away. Now the one who was asleep has woken up and is browsing a book on the castles of Wales; another nods off. Eventually the doors open and a member of the hotel staff appears with coffee, the only thing that seems at all likely to break the spell.

This first meeting is a glimpse of what is to come over the next couple of sessions. On the one hand, a gathering of Ex Men to discuss a series of pressing global issues and meet up with like-minded old friends. There are trips laid on – to the impressive Roman fortress and baths at Caerleon and, on the last night, a dinner at Cardiff Castle hosted by the First Minister of Wales (reading up on the castles of Wales suddenly seems like time well spent). Experts are brought in to the discussion sessions, but although the members listen, too many of them take these sessions as opportunities to expostulate rather than to produce new thinking. A conversation several years ago with one Ex Man in which they referred dismissively to the InterAction Council as the Inaction Council comes back into my mind at this point, as does that quip I promised to look up from the former Australian Foreign Minister Gareth Evans: 'relevance deprivation syndrome'. But despite this, some of the experts speaking are world-class, really impressive. And perhaps it's enough for them to be in the room, so that the Ex Men can absorb some of what they have to say, and regurgitate it later? When I ask former New Zealand Prime Minister Jim Bolger, a jovial, witty and perceptive presence throughout the three days, whether this whole occasion is just a talking shop or whether these groups of Ex Men get things done, he tells me it's a bit of both. 'One of the important realities that all former leaders have to accept, and I certainly have no difficult in doing so, is that your ability to direct is about nil – you're no longer in that position,' he explains.

So your real influence is how do you interact with people and perhaps persuade them to a slightly different position from the one
they were taking before. And some of that can perhaps be influenced by a discussion you've had with a half-dozen other people
in similar – or dissimilar – circumstances around the world. So
it's people of shared experiences, sharing time and debating issues
and then applying in whatever way they can the learnings from
those discussions. I mean, of course we formulate a carefully constructed communiqué and issue it to a wide range of people, but I
think the more important outcome would be the direct influence,
because they're all involved in some way and some manner in
their own countries, and you bring a different perspective from
the discussions.

In 2015, in the aftermath of a catastrophic outbreak of Ebola in west
Africa, that different perspective includes a focus on epidemic diseases and how to deal with them. The experts at the InterAction
Council have presented on topics including infectious diseases and
healthcare, and their thoughts are included in the communiqué.
The suggested action points include commitments to epidemic pre-
paredness, including creating and developing carefully maintained
stockpiles of personal protective equipment; targeted investment
and development effort at producing vaccines; increased funding
for global health security; and reform of the WHO, amongst other
things. If you'll forgive the pun, with the benefit of 2020 hindsight,
these do seem prescient. And when the Ex Men return to their
home countries, most could command some media attention for
ideas like these, if they marshal their message wisely. But Jim Bolger
is saying something more than that, and his analysis gets to a key
question in this chapter, and this book, which is about the nature

of influence. Is an Ex Man's 'power to persuade' greatest on transnational problems, with a global audience, or is it nationally, locally or perhaps even individually, in truly personal 'interactions'?

This book offers several different answers to that question, but for now there's another side to this annual meeting, of which the explosive confrontation between Zubkov and Yushchenko in front of the local students is just the first instalment. During the course of the next couple of days, and amid the fraternal chat over coffee, swanky dinners and trips to castles and Roman ruins, there is a sustained hunt for some progress towards a peace settlement, or at least a reduction of tensions, in Ukraine. This side of the event is driven by the chair of the InterAction Council, the former Canadian Prime Minister Jean Chrétien. Chrétien is, at eighty-one, still a sprightly and energetic figure. In recent weeks he has been busy: convening a seminar in Canada on Russia–Ukraine, attending a forum in Azerbaijan with three former Ukrainian Presidents, and then flying on to Moscow for a private meeting with Russian President Vladimir Putin. He invited Putin to send a representative to join the InterAction Council gathering, which is why Zubkov is here; Yushchenko, also invited to join these proceedings, was at the forum in Azerbaijan. Chrétien comes at this from a very particular angle: Canada has the world's third largest Ukrainian population, after Russia and Ukraine itself; and in the ethnic, linguistic and religious challenges facing Ukraine he obviously sees similarities with Canada. 'One area that we explored at the Ottawa meeting – and that I think as Canadians we understand well – is that it is possible to have a central government and regional autonomy, with language and religion guarantees, that work well,' a pre-council press release has him intoning. 'I believe this might be one way to help resolve the dispute in Ukraine.' In this spirit he has been approached to help Ukraine write a new constitution, and he is keen to involve other InterAction Council members who have relevant expertise. This, then, is how he introduces the session on Russia–Ukraine. Could the Canadian model be instructive here? It's important to begin dialogue even if people are very far apart. What can we do to help? He reveals a little of his conversation with Putin but acknowledges Putin told him nothing he hadn't already said publicly. And then the discussion begins. Except it really isn't a discussion at all: it's a stand-up row (or at least a sit-down one; these are old men, after all). On one side is Zubkov: shouting, lecturing and banging his fist on the table like a latter-day Khrushchev. On the other is Yushchenko, loud and equally passionate but able to keep himself – just – from shouting at the other Ex Men. Zubkov reels off all the usual Russian talking points, familiar to anyone who's watched five minutes from the months of wall-to-wall media coverage. This isn't of Russia's making, this is a Ukrainian problem; double standards are at play here; Russia is the victim. This point gets him so worked up that when he finishes, he has to wipe the spittle from his mouth; an adviser, sitting beside him, wears a broad grin throughout.

Yushchenko gives as good as he gets. Again there are the familiar arguments from countless TV and radio discussions, but his evidence is marshalled more effectively and his arguments are enrobed in the language of liberal democracy, of a rules-based global order, the better to appeal to this audience. Later, sitting in the sun outside the golf lodge with his translator between us, Yushchenko tells me he wishes the rest of the world would wake up to the danger that Russia presents, not just to Ukraine but to them too. 'There is this occupant who has lodged himself in Ukraine, an occupant who enjoys moving borders, who enjoys stealing other countries' lands, who absolutely ignores and neglects any international treaties and agreements. It's a dangerous country, Russia, which has put the wall between two countries and tears Europe apart.' When I ask him about the possibilities presented by this meeting with Zubkov, he surprises me. 'I don't really care what Zubkov thinks,' he says through his translator.

> He seems like a nice person, but he doesn't make any decisions. Prior to this meeting, within the last month and a half, I've participated in meetings in Baku and Riga and Oslo. And every time we're talking about the same thing. I've given dozens of interviews, just to try to go through this wall of Putin propaganda that has invaded the world in general. But I do believe we will win. I know that we have truth backing us up.

Yushchenko no longer has any formal position in Ukraine, but here he is, still trying to buttress his country's position and standing.

Back inside the conference room, sitting alongside him is Vaira Vīķe-Freiberga, a former President of Latvia who, after the Soviet invasion during the Second World War, was exiled for fifty-four years from her homeland. She has a habit of answering short questions with quite long, apparently meandering, but ultimately rich and satisfying answers. In London the day before the event in Wales, she was the standout contributor on a panel with several other distinguished Ex Men. Instead of answering directly a question about whether democracy is under threat, she related an elegiac story about visiting the UN building in New York during the Cold War, and how she longed one day to see the Latvian flag flying outside, along with all the others. Today she offers something similar, but more pungent. After reminding those around the table of what countries like hers went through to recover their independence in the immediate post-Cold War world, she discusses the betrayals of the Yalta conference at the end of the Second World War and the Molotov–Ribbentrop Pact at its start, some modern Ukrainian history, and finishes by saying that far from being the victim, Russia is behaving like the hypochondriac father in Molière's play.

•   •   •

'I told my friend Jacques Chirac, "You have a romantic idea of Russia – it's all troikas with bells and bearskin covers, romantically sliding in the snow, and Voltaire going to the Court of Catherine, and the grandeur of Tsarist Russia."' In exile, Vīķe-Freiberga was an academic who was interested in the intersection of memory, language and tradition. And talking to me just before the Russia–Ukraine session, she brings all that learning to bear in her analysis of how the West has, as she sees it, fallen for these Russian stories. 'We have a down-to-earth, painful experience of what both communism and Russian chauvinism can mean,' she continues:

> And it's different to the stereotypes that the West presents. The West tends to present Russia as a poor, ailing, sick relative – a rich uncle one should not annoy because one hopes for the inheritance. The Western leaders and the press seem to be constantly saying, 'We mustn't annoy Russia, we mustn't humiliate them.' But to humiliate 40 million Ukrainians seems to be OK.

The day before, I'd seen Vīķe-Freiberga embracing Yushchenko, and so I ask her about their relationship.

> Last time I was in Kiev we were supposed to have dinner at his

house, but he had to be taken urgently to hospital because his internal organs, his heart, has been seriously affected by that poisoning. And we recently had another case of somebody from the Russian opposition being poisoned, and [Alexander] Litvinenko in Britain. These are deliberate gestures to show the power that they have.

There is a gap here, not only between Yushchenko and Zubkov but between these Ex Men from Eastern Europe and some of the others in the room who seem to want compromise.

•   •   •

Back in the room, and once Zubkov, Yushchenko and Vīķe-Freiberga have made their contributions, something closer to a debate then plays out. There is some criticism of the way Ukraine has behaved; some of Russia; some attempt to balance, some to figure out what they can do. And then one Ex Man makes a pointed and specific suggestion instead: how about supporting the Organization for Security and Co-operation in Europe to monitor the border, and giving the organisation access to the whole of the conflict zone, so that we can have facts and not idle debate? This idea, which has the merit of being coherent, specific and offering something for the assembled Ex Men to say, receives widespread support and is included in the final communiqué.

The session has hardly been an exercise in harmony, but then again this issue is not very harmonious. At the end, Chrétien thanks everyone present. 'It's been quite a day,' he says, and for the first time Zubkov and Yushchenko both laugh. As the tension dissipates, Chrétien ends the session with the same question he started it with: 'What role can we play? I don't know, but we will do what we can.'

He says he'll go again to Ukraine and speak about the Canadian model, and says he's willing to go to Russia if they would find it useful. His enthusiasm is commendable, considering how draining the session has been. Not to mention dispiriting: we've ended with the Ukrainians restating their position, the Russians restating theirs, speaking past each other and with little to no variation from what either might have said in public, and a communiqué which does little more than endorse the already-agreed international plan. A couple of hours later, just before everybody heads out for dinner that evening, I bump into Jim Bolger in the hotel foyer, and we stop for a chat. He's interested in what I made of the session. I've seen this kind of negotiation before, away from the public gaze, but not with such high-profile figures involved, and I tell him I'm impressed with him and his fellow Ex Men. They've had to listen to a lot of obvious lies, endure some awful gaslighting and, because they think there's value in the dialogue, bite their tongues. Did you not want to say something about that, to call it out, I ask. Bolger smiles and shrugs. Perhaps it's the superglue rule again.

• • •

Ukraine isn't the only country on the agenda in Wales, nor the only subject where an Ex Man is making a forceful case for InterAction Council action. On the hotel balcony, surrounded by beautiful Welsh countryside, the council's most gregarious member, former Colombian President Andrés Pastrana, puffs on an enormous cigar and talks about the dark things happening in Venezuela. This conversation is taking place in 2015, well before Venezuela's total economic collapse, but almost fifteen years into the 'Bolivarian Revolution' under Presidents Chávez and Maduro. Whatever improvements there have been in equality and healthcare for the poor, political freedoms have been curtailed and civil society shrivelled, and Pastrana is campaigning with other Latin American – and Spanish – leaders for the release of political opponents of Maduro's government. 'We're very worried about what is happening in Venezuela,' he tells me. 'The world knows that there are political prisoners, that they are going after the media, not only starting trials of journalists but also expropriation of the media.' Pastrana started his working life as a journalist, and I get the sense that he feels this personally, as much as he understands its importance for a functioning democracy. But the bulk of Pastrana's activism on Venezuela has been in support of political prisoners held in jail or under house arrest. 'What we were doing is first of all showing the world that there were political prisoners in Venezuela. In January this year I went with President Calderón from Mexico and President Piñera from Chile to a forum organised by the opposition in Venezuela, to talk about democracy.' The three Ex Men wanted to visit Leopoldo López, an opposition leader who had been jailed after calling for anti-government demonstrations. But the visit didn't go as planned.

> We went the day that visits were allowed for family and for friends, and they did not let us in. They said, 'No, you have to ask permission, you need permission from the Foreign Ministry,' then they said, 'You need permission from the Defence Minister,' then they said we need the permission from the President. We said, 'We're here because it's the day in any part of the world when the family and friends can visit the prisoner.' 'No, no, no,' they did not allow us to go in.

Pastrana tells the story calmly, but in 1988 he was kidnapped by a drugs cartel and held for a week, and as he talks about the emotional toll on the families of López and the other jailed opposition leaders it's clear that this experience shaped him and gives him an emotional access to this issue. He told me about a conversation he had very recently with President Maduro.

I remember one day very late at night talking to Chávez, and I said to Chávez, 'Hey Hugo, how was your time in prison?' and he started telling me the story. And I said, 'Hugo, did they forbid your family to visit you?' 'Oh, no, no, no, my family was there, my wife and children.' 'And your friends?' 'Oh no, I had a special jail, special room, my family came to visit me. Andrés, you know one thing, I created my party in jail.' And I said, 'Did they humiliate you in any way?' 'No.' And he asked me, 'When you were kidnapped, Andrés, were you humiliated?' I said, 'Yes, you know I had to take my bath in the morning in front of everybody, and they were torturing me.'

It's a powerful story and Pastrana knows it.

So I asked him, 'President Maduro, Chávez had all the guarantees when he was in jail, and he did a coup d'état. Leopoldo and Daniel [Ceballos] didn't, they're not doing anything against democracy, so it's completely different. But he had all the guarantees – why don't you give the same guarantees?'

He will, I am sure, tell this story wherever and whenever he can. And it's obvious what he's trying to do. It's one thing for an NGO to issue a press release or hold a press conference about not being allowed access, but pictures of Ex Men being blocked when they try to visit a political prisoner are quite another. Using his access to the media to advocate for this issue, flag up the truth of what's happening there, the nature of the government, Pastrana has already been to the Club of Madrid and persuaded them to speak up; now he's in Wales to ask the InterAction Council to do the same. 'Oh yes. Absolutely. Both wives are really doing a good job. But we're trying to be also the political support for them.' Pastrana isn't alone; there have been dozens of initiatives over the years, but none of them has succeeded in shifting the Venezuelan government from a path which has led the country further and further into domestic chaos and international isolation.

Despite this seeming failure, I'm sure these Ex Men are doing more together than would be achievable alone. When I spoke to Kim Campbell, a former Canadian Prime Minister and at the time president of the Club of Madrid, she described this as 'convening power', the ability to persuade people to come together, which multiplies with more people involved. 'When you send out an invitation on Club of Madrid letterhead and they see all the names,' she explains, 'there's an instant credibility and respectability.' What Chrétien and Pastrana were looking to do was use this instant credibility and respectability, this convening power. Campbell herself points to the successful way in which the Club of Madrid has used its convening power – it's the largest organisation for Ex Men and currently counts more than 100 of them as members. In 2005, a year after the Madrid terror attacks, the club convened a global summit on democracy, terrorism and security, which produced a declaration called the Madrid Agenda. The principles and language it contained influenced international discussions at the time, including at the UN, EU and United States Senate. 'At a time when the American administration seemed to be taking the position that the rule of law was inconsistent with fighting terrorism,' says Campbell, 'it was a very important holding exercise until the administration changed, frankly. It gave a kind of aid and comfort and support to those who didn't accept the Bush administration's view, and in fact saw the dangers of that view in terms of the actual goal, which was to fight terrorism.'

Shades of a number of Ex Men's 'holding exercises' for those who don't accept the Trump administration's view. It's a pattern the club has followed since, with thematic programmes on a variety of global challenges, and fifteen years later, in the midst of the Covid-19 pandemic, club members again attempted to push back against a purely nation-state-level response. 'Stand-alone national strategies will not only prove ineffective in stopping the virus, but they would also mean that the international response will be weaker than needed to prove effective,' wrote former leaders from countries as varied as Senegal, Chile and Norway in an op-ed widely published around the world. Less clear is what impact all of this undoubted activity has had.

· · ·

So perhaps that Ex Man was only half-right to describe it as the 'Inaction Council'; it's just that we don't know what effect their actions have. Which is a very sharp contrast indeed from the third major club for Ex Men: The Elders. This one has, in a lot of different ways, been all about concrete ways of achieving measurable change. 'Part of the challenge, especially in the first couple of years, was trying to figure out, with them in the lead, and me trying to assist them in that process from behind, where could their collective efforts make the biggest difference. That is not as easy as it seems.' Mabel van

Oranje was the organisation's first chief executive. A phenomenon who had worked at the Open Society Foundations and married into the Dutch royal family, she is exceptionally well connected, smart and driven. 'Even if The Elders are united in their willingness to tackle a particular issue, is there space for people like them to make a difference on that issue?' she asks.

> So if you look at the area of peace-making – maybe the biggest challenge is peace-making in the Middle East. You have governments with entire teams working on that issue 24/7 for years and years. The Elders have a relatively small secretariat, so the question is if you want to contribute to peace in the Middle East, where can you make a difference?

Today, the answer to that same question comes through the organisation's elaborate 'theory of change'. This is both a core idea and a part of its strategic framework, describing not just which issues The Elders will address but how – in two specific ways – they hope to effect change. 'The first is to help improve the relationships between groups,' reads the key sentence; 'the second is to engage leaders more actively in The Elders' messages.' In short, use their convening power to bring groups together; and use their access to current leaders to lobby for change.

The organisation's history is wrapped up in this question of creating change. In late 2002, the billionaire British entrepreneur Richard Branson and his friend and collaborator the musician Peter Gabriel were discussing what looked like a steady march to war in Iraq. It seemed to them crazy to have a war to get rid of one person, Branson tells me by phone from his Caribbean island (I, meanwhile, am in the bowels of an anonymous office building in central London). So they contacted Nelson Mandela and asked him to see Saddam and persuade him to stand down, as you do. Branson says he and Gabriel thought Mandela was the only person with the moral stature to ask this question; Mandela agreed, on condition that UN Secretary General Kofi Annan went with him. The bombing started before the plan ever came to fruition, but it got Branson and Gabriel thinking. Mandela and Annan are powerful on their own, they reasoned; imagine what they could do together. And there lay the seed of The Elders. The two men hired a bevy of consultants to imagine what an organisation based around these two global leaders would look like and what it could do. They drew up a longlist of 100 potential members, Branson tells me. That list was given to Mandela, who then chose the first group, including Jimmy Carter, Mary Robinson and Martti Ahtisaari, the former Finnish President who won a Nobel Prize for his peace-making. Be sure to make clear that it was Mandela's decision, Branson urges me as the conversation comes to an end – they were appointed by Mandela. And over the years I've heard this repeated regularly by people at The Elders. Their moral authority comes from the collective moral authority of their members, but above all from the closest the world has had in recent years to a moral lodestar, a secular saint: Nelson Mandela. Mary Robinson, speaking from her home in western Ireland during the Covid-19 lockdown, tells me that she was originally quite sceptical about the idea, but then she sat down with the group, and with Mandela. 'I completely changed. I felt very seriously, "This is a mandate for life." And the way he spoke about it,' she recalls. Some of what he said that day is still on The Elders' website. Mandela read out a formal statement first.

And then he just spoke at the table. He told us, 'People wherever you go know more about their area than you do, so listen first, and be humble, but be independent and work for human rights. And reach out to those who are marginalised and young people and women and the poorest.' As far as I was concerned, as of that meeting I felt completely committed to doing whatever I could because I so admired him.

Much else about The Elders flowed from those early decisions. Conflict resolution would be a central preoccupation. The idea of village elders for a global village gave the organisation its name. Which in turn meant they couldn't hold significant jobs while being members: they had to be free to speak out. They'd try to supplement other organisations, not repeat what they were doing. Listening would be a constant. Forgotten issues and places would be a focus: in the first couple of years, they visited Zimbabwe and sought to broaden the narrative by focusing on the humanitarian crisis rather than political reform; they worked with young people on the divided island of Cyprus; they talked about the West's moral culpability for the almost total breakdown in Somalia. And above all else they used their influence together, as a collective. They would address issues of mutual concern, not pet projects. Decisions would be taken together. Members would visit together. They would speak out where necessary, and when they did, they would seek to gain as much publicity as possible.

But those early years were also about figuring out what they were really for, what they could usefully contribute. There was no such elaborate theory of change on the website then; but there were lots of pictures, many including Richard Branson. The question was whether they could bring all these institutional strengths and ideas to bear, or whether they would look an awful lot like the InterAction

Council but just with better-known Ex Men, Richard Branson – and his money.

The issue that really demonstrated what they could do, and how they could do it, was child marriage. In 2009, it was a marginal issue on the global agenda. Some organisations were working specifically to challenge the prevalence of child marriage, but more often the big players in the development business saw it as an offshoot of some other issue. Here it's undercutting the drive for universal education by keeping girls out of school, here pregnant thirteen-year-olds are causing a spike in maternal mortality, and so on. But more than that, according to Margaret Greene, a researcher and consultant on women's health who had been tracking the issue for some time and was called in to advise The Elders, few people understood the scale of the problem. 'It was really seen very much as a speciality issue,' she says, 'something that happens to a few girls under dramatic circumstances in limited locations.' This was the apparently unpromising state of the field when Mabel van Oranje arrived in it. As she describes it, The Elders were looking for issues where they could make a tangible difference. 'It had to be meaningful, and it made sense to do things that others couldn't easily do,' she recalls. They were interested in issues which had been forgotten because they were politically sensitive, or taboo, or just overlooked. And where they could use 'their moral voice and their authority and of course their contact books and their visibility to say, "OK, here's an issue that deserves more attention."' A crucial moment came at a meeting of the group in 2009 when Jimmy Carter said he wanted The Elders to speak up about the negative effects of religion on women. It was something he'd seen in his own life, he went on, and while religion and tradition are normally forces for good in the world, too often they are misused to justify discrimination against girls and women.

This was warmly received by the other Elders, and van Oranje and her team were tasked with finding a specific way for the group to contribute. Carter, meanwhile, penned a widely read newspaper opinion piece in which he discussed his 'painful and difficult' decision to leave the Southern Baptist Convention, after more than sixty years, over the church's teaching on the role of women. 'This view that women are somehow inferior to men is not restricted to one religion or belief,' he wrote.

> Women are prevented from playing a full and equal role in many faiths. Nor, tragically, does its influence stop at the walls of the church, mosque, synagogue or temple. This discrimination, unjustifiably attributed to a Higher Authority, has provided a reason or excuse for the deprivation of women's equal rights across the world for centuries.[2]

The piece received many positive responses from those grateful that someone in his position was prepared to speak out. 'But just speaking out on issues and making beautiful speeches and getting quoted doesn't necessarily change the world,' van Oranje tells me, bluntly, 'so we realised that we needed to find, in that broad gender field, an issue that is an example of how religion and tradition get misused too often. And then by pure coincidence we came across the issue of child marriage.'

Everyone else I've spoken to says this was far from pure coincidence, that van Oranje travelled and met with a range of organisations supporting girls and women, giving herself and her team the best possible chance to come across it. And indeed it was in these meetings that the issue of child marriage first emerged as a possible focus. Van Oranje has since devoted a large part of the past decade to this issue, first at The Elders and then at the offshoot NGO Girls Not Brides, but she still remembers her astonishment when she was first confronted with it.

At that time, I had personally worked on questions of development and justice and human rights for fifteen years, and I had never come across it. I had no clue about the size – 12 million girls per year, that's an enormous problem. And the impact – think how it relates to efforts to get all girls to school or reduce maternal mortality or reduce domestic violence. It's linked to eight out of the seventeen SDGs [Sustainable Development Goals]. So this is an enormously big problem, with enormously negative consequences, and yet it was being ignored.

Today, she reels off these facts and figures easily, but at the time she needed to reach out to experts in the field, eager for whatever data was available both about the scale of the problem and about what might be done to solve it. In time, she brought those experts in to address The Elders directly, who in turn readily agreed that this should be a focus. 'The Elders realised that they themselves could not solve this problem,' says van Oranje,

but what they could do was to make sure that this issue would get acknowledged globally. So, raise awareness about it, get it on the world agenda, make sure that when people in New York talk about girls' education, they are no longer ignoring the fact that a huge reason girls are out of school is they're pulled out of school to get married; that when they say, 'Let's reduce maternal mortality,' they realise that a thirteen-year-old child bride who's pregnant is at much higher risk to have complications or die in childbirth.

So it became a no-brainer: The Elders needed to get this issue spoken about. And of course they were uniquely well placed to do so.

And there was something else: The Elders' membership included not just Ex Men but also South African Anglican Archbishop Desmond Tutu and activist-advocate (and wife of Nelson Mandela) Graça Machel, so they could speak about these issues in a way that a group of Western development ministers never could. Mary Robinson, now chair of The Elders, thinks this combination of diversity and the quality of each member allowed for a different type of discussion. 'It is a privilege to be in that company,' she tells me.

I felt it from the very beginning. It's the quality of each of The Elders and now The Elders emerita that we have. Somehow people leave their egos at the door, or don't tend to have very strong egos. And the willingness to admit that we didn't know the scale of the problem, and that we understood that there were a lot of groups around the world dealing with this under the radar, because they were afraid to be too explicit, they were afraid of the cultural problems it might cause in their community, and therefore they were weaker in doing it than they otherwise would be.

But if it was clear there was a role here for the group in putting the issue of child marriage on the global political agenda and advocating for increased political commitment, expertise and money to address the problem, it was equally clear that ultimately change had to happen on the ground – in the lives of girls, their families and communities. And so the second decision was to found and incubate a separate organisation, which became the NGO Girls Not

Brides, to spearhead the campaign and specifically to coordinate work between all the organisations working on the field, and those who would be drawn into it. The third decision was that this would be the limit of their involvement. The Elders couldn't run this organisation or continue to lead the campaign; once they'd set it up and given it political momentum, their job was done.

Eleven years on, ending child marriage is now a target in the Sustainable Development Goals, the closest thing to a global to-do list. Many countries have legislated against child marriage; some have comprehensive strategies for ending it. Girls Not Brides has more than 1,400 member organisations in over 100 countries, holding those governments accountable and managing specific projects; foundations and governments have poured tens of millions of pounds into those projects. And everyone with whom I have discussed this history agrees that this would not have happened without the lead The Elders took back in 2009–11. I'll say more in the next chapter about how that was achieved, but for now it's enough to note that this campaign was a genuine and impressive achievement, and a tremendous early success for The Elders.

• • •

Six years after those meetings in New York on child marriage, six members of The Elders travelled to Moscow for a typically Elder-ish 'frank exchange of views' with top Russian leaders, including President Vladimir Putin. Far-right news site Breitbart News headlined its piece on the visit 'The Elders: Global Gallivanting Gasbags Who Refuse to Leave the Stage'.[3] It's a headline I've thought about a lot over the years, because I think it gets to two of the central questions of this book. First, and in its bluntest form: is it right? Are they…

gallivanting gasbags? The second question really boils down to a more polite version of the first: since their success with their campaign on child marriage, what equally concrete achievements have The Elders been able to chalk up? Mabel van Oranje left the group in 2012 after a family tragedy, and her idea of finding overlooked issues seems to have left with her. Today, The Elders' 'strategic framework' describes a focus on six enormous issues: encouraging ethical leadership, fighting climate change, averting conflict, changing the narrative around refugees and migration, advocating for universal health coverage and supporting access to justice. In a world where, as they put it, 'multilateral solutions to shared problems are in decline', this is a broad agenda. And across thirteen pages the document sets out how they will visit, write, meet, publish, convene, telephone and advocate on behalf of these causes. The Elders' theory of change largely involves their 'global reputation' and 'moral authority' doing the heavy lifting – for example, their work on universal healthcare will mean that, 'inspired and encouraged by The Elders' interventions, heads of state initiate, support and sustain major UHC [universal health coverage] reforms in their countries'. It seems far-removed from the intense pragmatism of the child marriage campaign; as Mabel van Oranje herself asked in relation to the Israeli–Palestinian conflict, how can one organisation, with a dozen members and a supporting secretariat of about twenty people, possibly hope to achieve meaningful change on massive issues like these which are already high up the global agenda?

There's a part-answer to both these questions in July 2013, a couple of days after US Secretary of State John Kerry has announced that long-stalled talks between Israeli and Palestinian negotiators will resume, in hopes of finally achieving a peace agreement. Visiting Washington, a delegation of Elders met Kerry to discuss the plan, then travelled to London, where they met UK Foreign Secretary William Hague, and now I'm waiting in a packed room at Chatham House, the venerable foreign affairs think tank, to hear what they will say publicly. It seems to me a pretty transparent effort to buttress Kerry's plan, and I'm surprised that they are acting essentially as outriders for US foreign policy; although it's also true that Kerry's plan is largely in line with the kinds of things they've been saying for years. And so here's the former Finnish President Martti Ahtisaari telling the audience of journalists, ambassadors and foreign policy experts that after their meetings in Washington, they are convinced that this is the only show in town. Coordination is vital to its success, he continues; this is the time for the Europeans to row in behind the US plan. Then Jimmy Carter chimes in, arguing that progress has been handicapped by the relative quiescence from Europe. And he reveals a little more of the details of the negotiations, claiming that both Israeli Prime Minister Benjamin Netanyahu (far from a noted Carter ally) and Palestinian President Mahmoud Abbas are ahead of their governments and need support. Finally, Lakhdar Brahimi, the former Algerian Foreign Minister who has been involved in countless peace processes and at the time is UN Special Envoy for Syria, argues that without support now, the very idea of a two-state solution will die. In my notebook, I write that 'the whole London foreign policy world comes to listen' – and if John Kerry can't be everywhere at once, what better way to get the message out to the countries the Americans need to be less 'quiescent' than by having Carter, Ahtisaari and Brahimi do it for you?

It's a noteworthy event for another reason. A couple of years earlier, The Elders appeared to go through a phase of reinvention. I heard rumours that Ex Men with the required moral fibre were in short supply, and if the focus was now on lending an ethical voice and conforming

to a certain set of global values, I could expect to see more appointments like Ela Bhatt, the Indian civil society activist who was involved
in the child marriage campaign, and the noted Pakistani human rights
lawyer Hina Jilani. The Chatham House event suggested the limits of
that approach – that when push comes to shove in political negotiations, political weight counts. But this question about how clean a potential Elder's hands are, versus their ability to reach those in positions
of power, remains relevant. A decade on from when she started at The
Elders, Mabel van Oranje still thinks about this dilemma.

When the group of people who are currently members of The
Elders were in power, they were almost untouchable. I, and many
in my generation, looked up to them, and we considered them
godlike. I guess that because of social media, potential new Elders
feel much closer to us. We know so much more about the next
generation of leaders. They feel more familiar, and we know more
about their flaws…

She thinks for a moment and then adds:

So I don't know to what extent this whole generation that you're
writing about is becoming extinct. There might not be a critical
mass of new candidates to join The Elders. Maybe there will never
be a sequel to your book, because the next generation of inspiring
global leaders is much younger. Look at Malala [Yousafzai] and
Greta [Thunberg]. It is fascinating that they have become icons
without previously holding formal positions of power.

It is fascinating, I agree, but she's not talking just about morality but
also about the ability to reach the public.

I remember sitting down with an American friend who ran an organisation working with millions of US teenagers to help these kids to do good for their communities and make a difference in their lives. We spoke about having those adolescents do something with The Elders. She looked at me and said, 'I am sorry to disappoint you. I am not sure that we can work together because I'd first need to explain who most of these Elders are.' She said that most average fifteen-year-old kids don't know who Nelson Mandela and Kofi Annan are. So she said, 'I'd prefer to work with Justin Bieber if I want my adolescent audience to do something.' … When you look at the people alive with the biggest name recognition in the world, I believe that you find Barack Obama and Michelle Obama in the top five, Malala is in the top five, and I guess that Trump is in the top five. All this shows us that power and privilege are relative, they change with different audiences in different places. That affects where and how prominent people can have an impact and make real change happen. As a result, The Elders might have to gravitate towards issues where they interact with a slightly more sophisticated audience. An audience that still respects the moral leadership of former statesmen and women.

The Elders' current CEO is David Nussbaum, and since Malala and Greta are certainly a bit young to be considered as Elders, when we sit down to talk I ask him about the other person on van Oranje's list: Barack Obama. They met him relatively recently, Nussbaum tells me, and had a good chat. He notes that Obama too is still quite young and perhaps has other things on his plate, before he heads off on a more comfortable tangent. But he does acknowledge that The Elders' star power is perhaps less than it was at the beginning: Kofi Annan, Jimmy Carter and Archbishop Desmond Tutu were globally recognised names; today, that's only true of former UN Secretary General Ban Ki-moon, hardly a dynamic presence in the way that Annan was.

The more important question is what they can achieve, though. And here Nussbaum offers some interesting insights. He acknowledges that the issues The Elders have chosen since child marriage don't lend themselves to van Oranje's approach – highlighting it and getting a campaign started before handing over to a more permanent team. Instead, the group now focuses on issues which are sometimes known as 'hardy perennials' – like garden plants, they can be trusted to keep coming back, year after year. Peace-making, universal health coverage and climate change are all worthy, but hardly susceptible to dramatic intervention in the manner of child marriage. And then there is the weight carried by that phrase 'inspired and encouraged by The Elders' interventions', about which I'm rather sceptical. Nussbaum gives me two cases where he thinks there's a chance their interventions did, if not exactly inspire, then perhaps encourage. The first was the example, as he puts it, 'of when nothing happens'.

In 2018, there was a great deal of concern at the prospect of violence during elections in Zimbabwe, and The Elders despatched Mary Robinson, Lakhdar Brahimi and Kofi Annan. It was to be Annan's last trip. 'He was worried about violence, and he wasn't feeling well,' Robinson recalls.

He was determined that he was going to do his best, and he was tireless in Zimbabwe. I think I only prevented him from staying at a civil society meeting that I could close for him, and to go back and have a rest before further meetings. And he got pneumonia on the way home and never recovered.

It was a tragic end to Annan's life and career, but the reason he persisted was because the chance of averting violence seemed real. The Elders met and got to know both the new President, Emmerson Mnangagwa, and his young challenger, Nelson Chamisa. They urged them, both privately and publicly, to encourage their followers to respect the process in general, and to cut out the attacks and threats against female candidates in particular. And the result, as Nussbaum puts it, was 'a small amount of violence … but frankly compared to what people were worried about there was very little violence'. He is quick to credit the Zimbabwean political leadership and people for their achievement. But? 'But we may have had a role in helping the Zimbabwean leadership and people achieve a peaceful election process and outcome.' Is it possible to pin that down to them, to their intervention? No. But?

> These were influential, respected African leaders, largely African Elders, speaking to people who would take note of what they said. And certainly there were steps taken following that call, about the way some women candidates were being abused. And I'm not aware of any other calls or highlighting that issue that happened. Now we can't prove anything; it may be somebody was already planning to do something, but it looks more than coincidence.

Nobody outside Zimbabwe heard, though, he says, because journalists don't report when there isn't a story.

Nussbaum's second example is half a world away: in Jakarta, Indonesia, in December 2017. Former Mexican President Ernesto Zedillo and former Norwegian Prime Minister Gro Brundtland went to see President Jokowi to talk about universal health coverage. And here my ears prick up, because this is the issue where 'inspired and encouraged' is supposed to happen. 'I don't know what President Jokowi was thinking, but he was certainly taking the meeting very seriously, he was very engaged,' Nussbaum begins. He argues that Zedillo would be seen as a peer – a former President of a country with a lot in common with Indonesia – a big, middle-income country with large economies nearby. Perhaps Jokowi would see in Zedillo 'somebody who has grappled with this kind of job in some kind of way'. Meanwhile, sitting alongside Zedillo was Brundtland, who has served as Director General of the World Health Organization, in the process seeing most countries' healthcare systems, and has also been a head of government. 'If that's who I've got speaking to me, I want to hear what they have to say and there's some level of connection and empathy that might not be there with different kinds of people.' And it's hard to argue with what Nussbaum's saying; it is easy to imagine that thought process. But what about measuring the outcome?

Nussbaum is very honest about this. There is no perfect mechanism. It is really hard. I sympathise, because that is the problem I have in writing this book. So I ask how he does it. He tells me he's developed a system of collecting anecdotes: when someone mentions to the team that someone was influenced by something they wrote, said or did, it's jotted down, and every six months it's tallied up in a spreadsheet. To me, this quixotic mechanism sounds a little like Islamic Hadith, the records of things the Prophet Muhammad said and did; they're graded according to who reported it, how close they were to the Prophet, how soon after his death it was recorded. In short, the closer to the source, the more reliable they might be. Religious scholars and NGO funders aren't really in the same game, though, and Nussbaum acknowledges the imperfection of his system. He's keen to stress that it isn't the way in which staff are judged – or else, human nature being human nature, people would just collect more anecdotes. But, he argues, collecting them is one way of understanding the impact of The Elders' behaviour. I can see that, but for me an equally important question is when, as with The Elders' child marriage campaign, you should stop doing something. When you should cut one of the programmes because it just isn't worth it. Nussbaum insists they do consider that. A couple of the current issues are slated for discussion, and might get dropped, at the end of the current cycle, he says. Although he adds that The Elders also don't like to make decisions like that too fast, and don't want to give up on something just because progress is slow. Which is fine, just as long as there's a difference between slow progress and no progress. Here, he uses another example to illustrate how this can happen, and why they think this way.

> I led a small staff visit to Israel–Palestine in 2017, and we had a meeting in the Knesset and we met with various civil society groups in both Israel and the Palestinian Territories. Our conclusion at that point, which we then reverted back to The Elders on, was it wasn't clear to us that there was an active public role for The Elders that was likely to make a positive difference at that time. That was a disappointing and frustrating conclusion to come to, but one of the things I've noticed about The Elders, and I have a deal of respect for this, is that they are prepared to do nothing and wait. And they also recognise that sometimes if you do something, that may preclude you from doing something else later.

Nussbaum is an experienced former head of a major international NGO, and he makes the point that some in the sector can get into a cycle of activity for activity's sake, and it's clear that he doesn't want

The Elders to be one of them. 'The fact that this is terrible does not necessarily mean that you should do your thing, now, there.' I think the question, if you're looking at it in a very hard-headed way, is whether The Elders as a group should continue to have any further engagement with this issue, or any others where they don't currently have 'an active public role for The Elders that was likely to make a positive difference at that time', as Nussbaum puts it.

•　•　•

At the hotel outside Dublin, the rain has stayed away, and as the American tourists head back out onto the verdant golf courses, GLF members and supporters are finishing up their breakfasts and heading over to a large conference room for two pretty packed days of geographically themed sessions. Unlike The Elders, the GLF doesn't have a programmatic approach to issues but exists to take the expertise of former leaders and make it available to current leaders. When I spoke to him in 2009, F. W. de Klerk described it as taking a leaf from the private sector:

> If they have a competent CEO, quite often that CEO will become the executive chairman of the board, and the next step will be to become the non-exec chairman of the board, and even after retirement, wise companies keep contact with people with insight and vast experience in the field of their activity. There is no such facility in government.

De Klerk told me that while it was important for a retiring President or Prime Minister to leave the stage, there is a price to be paid for such an approach. 'Quite often, especially in the developing world, new leaders find themselves quite alone, surrounded unfortunately by corrupt officials or by insufficiently trained officials,' he said.

If one makes a study, for instance, of what the IMF or World Bank demand from these developing states, they simply don't have the infrastructure or the capacity which are required by these conditionalities imposed by international institutions. It is there that I think we can be of great value to leaders in countries who need advice, who need to take initiatives. And my focus, and our focus, is not to say, 'What are you doing wrong?' but to say, 'What initiative do you have to take to change the image of your country, what initiative do you have to take to build investor confidence, what initiative do you have to take to further democratise successfully, what must you do to uphold the rule of law, what must you do in your fight against corruption?'

Sir Robin Christopher, the GLF's first chief executive, told me once that de Klerk 'does believe in the power of personal advice'. So perhaps it's no surprise that the idea for the foundation originated with a friend. Graham Barr, a former journalist and one-time oil executive, suggested it to de Klerk after he'd witnessed both the transition planning in the corporate sector and the travails of political leaders struggling with the loneliness of power. When I spoke to him before his death, Barr told me that de Klerk had understood the concept immediately: 'He'd been isolated too, like they all are.' But he also told me that confidentiality was absolutely vital. 'If anyone wants to showcase, it's not the place. It's an organisation about doing serious work seriously.' And when I asked de Klerk about what can sometimes seem like an obsession with confidentiality, he offered me this explanation: 'It's not because we're a secret organisation – we have a website and everything – but because we don't want a loss of face for the leaders that we advise. We leave it to them to disclose to what extent would they like to make it public that they associate with us.' Very few have, but there do appear to be quite a few projects. Even back in 2009, only five years after the GLF was established, de Klerk told me that they had advised two countries in Africa, one in the Middle East and one in Eastern Europe, while today their website cryptically lists a number of other projects which have taken place over the intervening decade.

Of the projects they do discuss, perhaps the highest-profile is in Mozambique, where the former Botswanan President Sir Ketumile Masire led teams on a number of visits over three years (2013–16) and then co-chaired international mediation talks. The GLF team – all of whom had deep previous ties to Mozambique – privately advised two Presidents, Armando Guebuza and his successor Filipe Nyusi, before Masire took on the more public role. From the outside, the situation seemed tailor-made for bargaining and mediation of this kind: as Dr Alex Vines, of the Chatham House think tank, wrote in an assessment for the UK government's Stabilisation Unit, Mozambique had a history of deals between the two sides' high commands, with military and political insurgency used tactically for political ends, rather than developing spontaneously at local level, and was therefore more amenable to political deals than in some conflict situations.[4] The peace process did eventually produce an agreement, but not until 2019, and when I call him to discuss GLF's role, Vines is much more circumspect about how tailor-made it was.

My conclusion is that the Mozambican peace process probably needed organisations like the GLF ... and others, but it moved forward actually by the mistakes they made, convincing the Mozambicans that they didn't need foreigners in that way, [or] multiple mediators. It brought the RENAMO leader, before he died, and President Nyusi together to realise they needed to cut out mediators and talk to each other directly. So it's the failure of that process that contributed to moving it forward.

In their summary, the GLF are careful not to claim credit for the eventual success of the process, noting instead that they 'helped ease tensions around a presidential transition, build trust in dialogue between the government and the main opposition party that had boycotted elections, and co-chaired mediation talks leading to direct talks between the President and leader of the opposition'. But Vines thinks really acknowledging the failure is a pretty hard sell for any organisation making the case for its own continued existence. 'They portray it as a positive success, but actually I think the history will show the opposite. But it was still really important that they did what they did.' It's an interesting spin on failure – like the Silicon Valley mantra of 'failing fast, failing forward'. As Joe Clark, a former Canadian Prime Minister who has conducted many projects for GLF, puts it, although not specifically referring to Mozambique, 'There's another reality about the work that we do. It's like any organisation dealing with quite difficult issues: we fail more often than we succeed.'

Elsewhere in Africa, the GLF worked to ease political tensions in Ghana in 2013–14 and supported Kenya's Elections and Boundaries Commission in 2011–13. They worked with the Club of Madrid in Haiti in 2011 after the earthquake, and with the United Nations, amongst others, in post-independence Timor-Leste in 2007–09. In Timor-Leste, the GLF chose two Ex Men, both hailing from small island nations: Mike Moore, the gregarious former Prime Minister of New Zealand, and Cassam Uteem, a former President of Mauritius.

The team was rounded out by the GLF's Sir Robin Christopher, who had been a former British Ambassador to Indonesia and was therefore well acquainted with both the region and the specific challenges facing Timor-Leste. They were asked to suggest reforms to the staffing and structure of the office of President José Ramos-Horta. When I ask him about this more than a decade later, Uteem gives me a valuable insight into how the GLF does business. 'President Ramos-Horta was the first one to realise that his office was completely disorganised, not to say a real mess, and required outside expertise to make it functional. He was ready to listen to our suggestions,' he begins. Uteem lists some of the changes they recommended – whether it was an organisational chart, funding for overseas trips or more structured relations between his advisers. But how did the visiting Ex Men build trust, in a very short period of time, with Ramos-Horta, which would be crucial if he was to accept them into his confidence and then consider their recommendations? '[It] was made easy for me,' Uteem explains, because the leader of his Mauritian political party had been a rare supporter of Ramos-Horta when times were tough.

It didn't require much more than that for us to establish a relationship based on trust that was crucial for an open, frank and honest exchange of views. He was also an experienced diplomat and it didn't take him long to be convinced that the GLF and members of the mission had no hidden agenda.

Although the GLF project team had prepared detailed briefings before they travelled to Timor-Leste, it wasn't until they met the President and Prime Minister that more mundane machinery of government issues arose. But how helpful does Uteem think Ramos-Horta found their recommendations?

I know for sure that the President expressed open appreciation, not to say gratitude, to the GLF team(s) for what he described as sound advice tendered to him, some on a one-on-one basis, very informally, and which didn't appear in the original terms of reference or in the reports of the Missions.

I think that last point gets to the heart of what the GLF offers: an opportunity to sit with people who have had responsibility at the highest level and experienced the loneliness of power, to just chew the fat, to ask some other questions – 'How do you deal with this?', 'What happens if you do that?' It's too attractive not to take advantage of. Uteem has been more open than anyone else I've spoken to, but this is where the door closes. Although there is a coda: José Ramos-Horta left office in 2012, and shortly afterwards joined the GLF. And in the years since, offering this type of advice has been a growing business: The Elders and the Club of Madrid have moved into it too, albeit in different ways. The Club of Madrid was also involved in Timor-Leste's democratic transition, and after leaving office José Ramos-Horta joined their organisation too. They've also worked on democratic transitions in Tunisia, on security sector reform in Serbia, and 'facilitating a political consensus' in Bolivia. And they namecheck Bolivia, Ecuador, Kyrgyzstan, Myanmar and Haiti as beneficiaries of a variety of projects aimed at encouraging democratic transition.

But while all the organisations concerned play their cards close to their chest, none is quite so discreet as the GLF, perhaps because none exists solely to offer one-on-one, peer-to-peer advice to heads of state and government. Still, speaking to other members at the annual meeting and in the months since, more emerges about the organisation's modus operandi. How do they find new business, for one? 'We usually have to alert potential heads of government as to what we do,' Joe Clark says. 'Our very discretion does not make us visible, and so we have to find ways – often through intermediaries – where someone who knows one of us or knows about the organisation will suggest that perhaps there's an interest in a conversation.' As he tells me this, sitting in the side-lines of a session at the annual meeting, he's surrounded by potential intermediaries: men and women with interests and connections spanning the globe. But even if a project is agreed, it doesn't always turn out as expected. 'Sometimes a leader comes to us knowing he is uncertain about a certain area and will ask our advice, and the question which we were invited to address turns out not to be the question we end up addressing,' Clark tells me. 'In some cases that's because on reflection the head of government in question thinks that he doesn't really want advice on that, but as often the conversation leads that person to think of something else on which he does need advice.' Just like Cassam Uteem and José Ramos-Horta in Timor-Leste. Regardless of where the conversation may go, the trip will be meticulously planned. Sometimes (as in Mozambique) existing relationships are built on; if not, there's an expectation that the President's advisers will have done their research on the visiting team; often there will be multiple meetings over the course of several days. Ex Men stress the importance of listening, and understanding the President or Prime Minister's circumstances, not trying to impose something unachievable on them. When composing a team, it's clear the GLF secretariat search hard for the best possible match, despite Joe Clark's observation that these conversations often head off in unexpected directions. I always imagine it's a little like F. W. de Klerk going through his rolodex to find an Ex Man who's had just that challenge, and then sending them. And when I put that to Lawrence Gonzi, the former Maltese Prime Minister, who was chosen for a mission to an unnamed African country, he concurs. Firstly, he says,

> Certain aspects of the economy of this particular country were familiar to me in Malta. And second, there was a particular issue related to the technical aspects of the rules regarding how a general election was administered. Why do I mention this? Because if you look into my biography, way back when I was Speaker of the House of Parliament in Malta I had chaired a commission trying to help both sides to review the electoral process in Malta in order to avoid a constitutional crisis.

Did the Prime Minister find the advice useful, I ask, and were the recommendations implemented?

> Yes, certainly the person concerned did appreciate the recommendations. But we realised as well, and we had already warned him, that in this aspect – not in other aspects where I know they were successfully implemented – that for them to be implemented they needed a national agreement, cutting across party politics. And I know how difficult that is.
>
> I myself, when I had chaired this commission in Malta, achieved perhaps 60 per cent of what needed to be done, and it took months of patient cajoling and massaging to get the two sides to agree 60 per cent, so I had warned this person that these recommendations needed the whole country to embrace them. Otherwise, if forced down somebody's throat the result would be the other way around. And, as far as I know, that level of consensus has not been reached.

There's a level of empathy here which might be very different if the same advice came from a British or French politician. And there's also the importance of listening to the unique circumstances of the country and not trying to impose something, Gonzi explains.

> We understand that we might suggest, but at the end the reality is the reality in your country, not in our country. We could make suggestions, from our previous experience, without any political bias at all, and this is the advantage of GLF. You know that there's no hidden agenda, this is exclusively for the ears of the person in office, and the person in office can do whatever he or she likes with what we say. He or she could implement what we recommend, or just discard it completely, and nobody is going to get criticised.

At the annual meeting in Dublin there is a bit of muted criticism, though. Not of failed projects, because no one is given enough information to judge one way or the other, but during the meal and coffee breaks there's some muttering from attendees who would like the GLF to be a bit more forthcoming with the details. And there's a sense that the discussions have been a bit of a downer, with endless sessions dissecting the world's problems in enormous detail. I don't really understand this myself: this is an organisation devoted to fixing those problems, not arranging tours of the happy factory. But could they offer some more detail? It's hard to see how. At the start of each session, the project director gives a short *tour d'horizon*, mentioning countries where the GLF either has a project or has discussed a project, or where they sense there might be opportunities. Any more than that, and the confidentiality begins to break down. But you don't have to listen long to one of these sessions – with panels of Ex Men and contributions from the floor – to find their real value: simply amazing insight. Several members have recently been UN Special Representatives of various descriptions, many are actively involved in various peace initiatives, all travel widely, and a few are able to distil a lifetime's worth of experience into stunningly illuminating contributions. To hear Lakhdar Brahimi discuss the Middle East, in detail and without a filter, for example, is like having your eyes opened anew. Joe Clark, former Jamaican Prime Minister P. J. Patterson, former New Zealand Prime Minister Helen Clark and de Klerk himself all bring insight, and while contributions from the other attendees – supporters, funders and hangers-on – do vary in quality, some of them share nuggets of rare intelligence. I can see how all these offerings, together with the more private conversations afterwards, help the GLF identify and assess potential opportunities that they hadn't previously been aware of. More important still, perhaps, is the web of personal connections which might bring an introduction, and an opening.

•   •   •

And then there's the question of money. When I spoke to her in 2011, Kim Campbell, the former Canadian Prime Minister and at the time head of the Club of Madrid, was in a frustrated mood. 'I was a bit annoyed when The Elders was created because Richard Branson came along with $25 million to create this organisation,' she says. 'I keep thinking, "Oh gosh, if somebody had given us $25 million we'd be infinitely more productive than we are now."' As she explains the reasons, her frustration reminds me of the fundraising challenge many NGOs face: 'At the Club of Madrid, we have no trouble getting money for projects; the core funding is always a challenge.' I think there are two ways to consider the money these organisations raise, and spend. Kim Campbell's is the first, and it fits with the rest of this chapter: is this money being well spent? Could it, spent elsewhere – on guinea worm or house-building or a hundred other things – be doing more good? From my conversations, it's clear that The Elders' work on child marriage moved the dial on that issue, in all sorts of ways. Perhaps most importantly, when I asked simply whether ending child marriage within a generation would have been incorporated in the UN's Sustainable Development Goals without them, Margaret Greene answered simply, 'No.' That money probably couldn't have been spent better elsewhere; and since then David Nussbaum is convinced that their new model, focusing on the 'hardy perennials', continues to achieve real change, but absent his anecdotes about elections in Zimbabwe and universal health coverage in Indonesia it's hard to provide the receipts, as it were.

For the GLF, it's even trickier. Their modus operandi, layered on top of the inherent difficulty of identifying cause and effect in any political system, means results are almost impossible to demonstrate, and certainly not publicly. Mabel van Oranje, always focused on concrete achievements but working in a field where nebulous influence is often at play, assessed it this way:

You know how individual encounters can make a huge difference in our lives. And so, if the group has made ten trips to go advise sitting Prime Ministers and Presidents and their advice has been ignored nine times … but if once, on the basis of just one conversation, a leader decided to do the right thing instead of the wrong thing, that could really have had a catalytic leverage effect that we're not aware of. That's why I find it so difficult to judge all these things.

I do, too. The GLF has spent a lot of money – about £1 million a year – a lot of time, and a lot of airmiles trying. Money, time and airmiles which could have gone into something concrete. But what if it has paid off? It feels to me like a bet, or a Silicon Valley venture capitalist carefully investing in a dozen companies in the hope that one big success justifies the other failures. And if the Ex Men involved donate their time for free, what's the harm?

But there's a second way of thinking about funding, which asks a series of questions about whether fantastically wealthy people are able to buy access to power and influence through Ex Men; and about whether buying that access sometimes allows people with less than spotless reputations to launder them. Kim Campbell again, I think, captures the broad view of most of the Ex Men and their organisations I've spoken to: 'They're not really getting that much access with us – I don't worry about it too much because we don't have any power.' Nevertheless, the GLF annual meeting was full of people interested in what the Ex Men had to say. Some of these names are in the public domain – wealthy private individuals, companies with interests in mining or oil or finance, and some partner organisations with intersecting interests; others are not. Over the course of the meeting I met people in all those industries who clearly found the meetings very useful for the way they thought about their investments in developing countries. They weren't getting very detailed, specific information from the public sessions, but I wondered what was happening in those private conversations. And so, a couple of months after the meeting, I sit down in a bustling co-meeting space with Sir Robert Fulton, the GLF chief executive. A former Commandant General of the Royal Marines who later served as Governor of Gibraltar, he tends to answer questions directly, so I hope he does today, because the last time I asked about the GLF's finances was in that meeting with F. W. de Klerk all those years ago. Then, the organisation was still relatively young and idealistic. 'We have decided not to opt for the easy way of getting three or four corporations to give us enough money for our whole budget, because then there could be a suspicion that we are actually representing their particular interests in the developing world,' de Klerk told me then. 'We chose to go for smaller donations from more companies, more foundations and the like, so that we can be totally independent and really offer to the governments we advise this objectivity, not speaking on behalf of anybody, not promoting the foreign policy of any other country, but advising them.'

Ten years on, Fulton tells me that rule has been further embedded.

The largest donation we would ever accept in a single year is one tenth of our annual expenditure, of give or take £1 million a year. We have never got anywhere near that and nor do we seek to. The reason for that is quite obvious: that we do not wish to be beholden to anybody, either that the donor might tell us what to do, or they might blackmail us by saying, 'If you don't do this, we won't support you any more,' and all of a sudden there's a massive hole in our budget.

In the early days most of the donors were friends of de Klerk, people who admired him and wanted to support his work. Today, Fulton says they are still an important part of the mix, but they have been joined by companies and individuals, often working in developing countries, and with a long-term financial interest in stability; and more recently by people invited to join the GLF network for what they might bring to it. Which all sounds jolly good, except stability can mean all sorts of things, and networks based on mates' recommendations don't always have the best vetting processes. But then he tells me something which surprises me with its candour. 'If one of these people suggests somebody, and it has happened within the last ten days, and I had to say, "I don't want you to pursue that," because I don't think they would be suitable.' He says red flags might include companies with too-strong links to a single country or companies offering to donate if the GLF ever does a project in a specific country. And in these cases, 'it's not only the probity question but it's also to what extent might it break our confidentiality', by giving details to that company in order to unlock the promised cash. But even if a company, or an individual, is above board, aren't GLF's wealthy donors still paying for undue access? Fulton reaches for the same argument as Kim Campbell, noting that his members aren't people still in power, and he makes a rather unsubtle, but nevertheless accurate, jab at the World Economic Forum, by pointing out that wealthy donors do get to hobnob with sitting heads of government in Davos. But after my experience at the annual meeting, he also makes a broader point about the nature of the GLF network:

> I'd also say these conversations go both ways. There are business-
> es with interests in various countries, and one reason we do the
> meetings in that way is that lots of this information comes back
> the other way. If you're the head of a business in a country, you
> may have good links into that country to today's leaders, and
> we can benefit from that by way of introductions, so this is very
> much two-way.

In a world where foreign aid is reducing and foreign direct investment (FDI) from companies is increasing, Fulton argues that it's also a good thing for companies to know more about the country in which they're thinking of investing, so they can make better decisions: so conversations like these can be valuable both to the company and to the country. 'I understand that somebody might misuse something they've heard or learned. I think that's a risk they take; if we heard about it, we'd do something about it. I've never seen something which has given me cause for concern in the ten years I've been here.'

Another area seems much trickier to me: what if one of his Ex Men members has a conflict of interest? How does he guard against that? His answer isn't immediately reassuring. 'Really by knowing the members themselves. The forty-five members we have at the moment choose whoever follows,' and any one of them can effectively blackball a new member. 'The reputation of all forty-five is only as good as the weakest reputation of the forty-five. Therefore they won't allow anyone to join about whom any of them have any doubts.' Fulton notes that this wouldn't necessarily prevent a conflict of interest, but he adds that since the Ex Men are never alone during their country visits – a member of the secretariat is always there – it should be practically impossible. And then that burst of honesty again. 'I think we would pick it up. And, actually, we have picked one up, but it had not got as far as a project. It was a suggestion.' He says that when members suggest very specific projects this is one question to ask.

Where you get to issues that are associated with enabling and encouraging FDI, you come quite close to some of those, in the sense that if you're trying to create conditions for people to invest in a country. I mean, we've had questions about mining licences from some of the companies, and we declined to get involved in a discussion with a country about the allocation of mining licences, because it was quite apparent that one of the companies that was then on our list was going to benefit directly from the discussions which might follow.

So you declined that? 'We declined.'

Depending on how you feel about politicians, about the elite, about corporations and corruption, you might have a number of different responses to this burst of openness. But I think it's unusual for someone operating in this elite world to speak so candidly not just about the risks of corruption but about its appearance. One reason I think Fulton feels comfortable with this degree of transparency (and he hasn't named the organisations or individuals, so I can't confirm what he's told me) is that the GLF is structured around giving advice for free. When a team goes to visit a country, the Ex Men – apart from a per diem – don't get paid. I ask if this is designed to protect the reputation of the GLF and its members.

We approached it from the opposite direction, which is that when the organisation was set up, it was set up as an altruistic way for people who had experience and were willing to give it to do so, full stop. In order to implement that philosophy, what rules do you need? So, I think I'd start with the philosophy rather than the rules.

You don't hear about altruism very much these days, particularly not where politicians are concerned, but I think I've seen quite a lot of it amongst the Ex Men I've interviewed for this book. All the members of the GLF can and do earn substantially more elsewhere. 'I have to compete for their time,' Fulton tells me later in our conversation. 'I know in some cases I'm competing with people who are paying them to do things. So they have to want to come and do it for

GLF.' Amazingly, this includes supporting Fulton with the hard slog of fundraising. Some of the members help out with the corporate supporters – doing lunches or dinners, seminars or speaking as part of a management training programme. With just a year's money in the savings account, Fulton believes this process keeps the organisation tight and focused on impact and value. And then he says, 'So I want members to work for the money.' Which they don't get paid? 'Yes.' And he chuckles.

The Elders have a slightly different model, but not so very different, and without the fundraising slog. They have a smaller number of donors on their advisory council, each making very large donations. Generally they're foundations or wealthy philanthropists, and since the organisation's inception they've been remarkably stable. Like at the GLF, donors get to join the annual retreat and hear The Elders' thinking, analysis and insight. And, rather like my experience in Ireland, this is often very high-level. As David Nussbaum puts it, 'It's an extraordinary privilege for the advisory council, and indeed for me, to see the distillation of experience and expertise and wisdom into a view, a decision, a perspective, an action, and it's not often you get the chance to see that in action.'

• • •

'Unfair trials were commonplace, particularly in politically motivated proceedings, during which suspects were typically detained and charged without access to a lawyer of their choice,' reads Amnesty International's latest summary about Azerbaijan.

Leading human rights organizations remained unable to resume their work … All mainstream media remained under effective government control … The authorities continued to arbitrarily arrest and detain independent journalists and bloggers … The authorities intensified their clampdown on critics who had fled the country, and unlawfully transferred many of them back to Azerbaijan and harassed their families.

On and on it goes. And yet for ten years I've been receiving newspaper alerts popping up to inform me of regular, often repeated, visits to Azerbaijan by a variety of Ex Men. I was curious to know what they were doing there: bearing in mind the circumstances, was this a case of an exaggerated faith in one's ability to effect change? One of the frequent visitors is Vaira Vīķe-Freiberga, so furious about the behaviour of Russia in Ukraine but not so furious, it seems, about the behaviour of Ilham Aliyev, President of Azerbaijan since 2003, in his country. And it's not as though any of this is a secret confined to the Europe and Central Asia subsection of the Amnesty International website. In January 2015, the *New York Times* editorial board felt moved to write about Aliyev's two faces, noting that while he is suave, speaks good English and promotes a moderate and modern form of Islam, nevertheless 'his authoritarian regime has one of the world's worst records on human rights'. The *Times*'s editorial board recognised the choice Western policymakers faced between interests and values, but it concluded with a recommendation:

The West must understand that the authoritarian Mr. Aliyev is the real Mr. Aliyev. As he accelerates his campaign to crush opponents and any other semblance of freedom, the United States and Europe should make far clearer than they have that while they may be compelled to do business with him, they have no illusions about what he is and the severe damage he is doing to his country.

I quote that because the previous year had seen a spate of Ex Men visiting Azerbaijan. In March, the former French Prime Minister Dominique de Villepin was in the capital, Baku, to congratulate Azerbaijan on its economic growth. In April, the former Israeli Prime Minister stopped in to discuss the possibilities presented by the Global Shared Societies Forum, to be held later that year. In October, the forum itself attracted Ex Men from several countries including Italy, Estonia and Latvia, and in December it was the turn of former Serb President Boris Tadić, getting started on plans for the next forum.

Central to much of this activity is Baku's Nizami Ganjavi International Centre, which boasts several Ex Men – including Tadić and Vīķe-Freiberga – on its advisory board. I assume they're all there to encourage Aliyev's pro-Western sympathies, and to encourage the democratic process. But is there a danger they get the balance wrong, instead offering legitimacy to an autocratic regime? 'It's certainly a danger, but what strikes me as a very curious thing is that these considerations, which are quite logical, seem to apply to small countries and not to large,' Vīķe-Freiberga tells me when I ask her this question directly.

> I see everybody and his dog trotting off to Moscow. I seem to remember [former Libyan dictator Muammar] Gaddafi being received in the Élysée and pitching his tent on the lawn there because he had a lot of oil and because [former French President] Mr Sarkozy was hoping to get him involved in his Mediterranean project. There seem to be two categories of people: those with natural resources that one needs or nuclear weapons in their arsenal, and those one can quite happily visit and interact with and no one will ever reproach you for having supported their

regime. But smaller countries like Azerbaijan do get this very strict examination.

I'm not sure this is completely accurate, both because everyone understood the nature of the Gaddafi regime and because Azerbaijan does have energy resources. And I wonder whether she has a blind spot – perhaps because of her and her country's history – for countries like Azerbaijan which have emerged from the shadow of Russia. 'A country like Azerbaijan has its pluses and minuses,' she says.

What attracts me is it has managed to do the transition to the post-Soviet period and its independence because it does have its own natural resources. It has managed to survive despite losing huge territory to Armenia thanks to the Russian intervention in favour of Armenia and the conflict in Nagorno-Karabakh, which I'm sure was planned by Russia as a way of keeping these two countries at each other's throats and preventing them from becoming too independent, and what the Russians would consider going out of their sphere of influence. What impresses me about Azerbaijan is that despite clearly seeing a population that is largely Azeri but is nonetheless multicultural, and has different religions represented, the Muslim majority is not a fundamentalist one. The separation of religion and state is very strictly observed. I have myself accompanied the President at openings of a Christian church, visiting a synagogue that the government had constructed. This is an example to a great many countries that Western leaders have no compunction in visiting and being seen as ideologically supporting, where there is a great deal of intolerance towards other religions, where churches get burned down, where people get massacred for being the wrong sect, even. So this, I feel, is very much to be encouraged.

It is only at the end of this rather long description of all that is to be admired about Azeri culture and society and the President himself that she gets to the potential negatives. 'But of course the imprisonment of journalists and various civil society representatives, we do try as much as we can to convince the powers-that-be that being open to them would be better for the country's prestige than any number of foreign dignitaries that come and visit them.' The President doesn't appear to have been convinced, and in fact so central has attracting foreign dignitaries to Azerbaijan been that it has been given a name – 'caviar diplomacy'. In its 2012 report on the phenomenon, the European Stability Initiative think tank pointed to its effects on various European MPs working with the Parliamentary Assembly of the Council of Europe (PACE). The report detailed the gradual tempering of criticism in election monitoring reports, and a group of members sympathetic to Azerbaijan despite the obvious democratic deficiencies, and suggests that this was driven in part by corruption; a later independent investigation on behalf of PACE concluded that 'there was a strong suspicion that certain current and former members of PACE had engaged in activity of a corruptive nature'. No one I have spoken to suggests that this is the case with the Ex Men who visited Azerbaijan, but there does seem to be a different calculation at play here. Azerbaijan doesn't have loads of extremists, and they're not exporting terrorists or migrants. In other words, they're not causing us any problems, so let them be.

•   •   •

In December 2013, the Club of Madrid organised a conference entitled 'Jobs for inclusive growth: A call to the G20'. It was hosted by Wim Kok, the former Dutch Prime Minister and at the time president of the club. Twenty-one other Ex Men are listed as attendees,[5] as are representatives from the Australian government, the World Bank and the International Labour Organization (the UN body dealing with jobs and employment). They were joined by dozens of ambassadors, think-tankers and of course the seemingly omnipresent representatives from the Nizami Ganjavi International Centre. At a hotel in Australia, this high-powered group spent two days discussing topics such as 'Job-Rich Growth', 'A Focus on Youth', 'More Jobs, Less Poverty', 'Green Jobs' and plenty of other buzzy-sounding subjects.

But if you look more closely, and you know what you're looking for, something about this meeting seems very odd. For a conference about jobs, there aren't that many representatives from the private sector; except for those who work for Mineralogy or Queensland Nickel. For a gathering of such senior political figures, ostensibly to feed into the Australian presidency of the G20, there are very few Australian politicians, except eleven from one small, recently formed political party. There's the unexpected location – a resort hotel just north of Brisbane. And then there's the name – the Club of Madrid is now working alongside something called the World Leadership Alliance (or WLA). The joint general secretary of the WLA writes in his welcome letter that the new organisation will 'bring together seasoned political leaders from the Club de Madrid – all democratic former Presidents and Prime Ministers – and corporate leaders from the World Economic Council to address some of the world's most pressing challenges'. The man who wrote those words is Clive Palmer, a bombastic mining tycoon who has long aspired to a bigger role in public life. Palmer was also the president of the World Economic Council. Mineralogy and Queensland Nickel, the event sponsors? Both owned by Palmer. The resort hotel, at Coolum Beach… well, another part of Clive Palmer's empire, of course. And the politicians, some of whom, including Palmer, had recently been elected to the Australian Parliament, represented, yes, the Palmer United Party. The journalist who first joined up the dots of this puzzle is Hedley Thomas, and when I speak to him a couple of years later he still sounds amazed at what the Club of Madrid allowed itself to be drawn into – providing what he describes as a 'sheen of credibility' and a 'platform for Clive to promote himself'. I'm certain this isn't the image that the world's largest group of Ex Men wants to be projecting, so surely they should have done more to assure themselves that the co-chair of their new organisation wasn't just trying to promote himself? When I asked the club whether they conducted a due diligence exercise, a spokesperson replied to say that 'before any activity or collaboration WLA-CdM conducts a serious due diligence exercise'. Has it conducted a due diligence exercise on Clive Palmer since then? 'Due diligence exercises are part of our work and a frequent practice particularly when it comes to donors. Please note that Mr Palmer's support ceased in 2016.'

I bet it did. Because while Clive Palmer was gadding around with Ex Men on the Gold Coast, donating hundreds of thousands of pounds to the World Leadership Alliance and Club of Madrid, his business was in severe distress and a couple of years later collapsed into administration. Meanwhile, the World Economic Council, set up as a way for businesses to give money to the Club of Madrid, but which the club concedes 'never actually took off', was 'formally terminated' in 2017. Bearing in mind this history, should other organisations be a little wary when considering partnerships with the Club of Madrid? This question is particularly relevant because in July 2019 the Commonwealth announced that it had secured an agreement with the club which 'commits the two organisations to work in closer partnership to promote peace and good governance in the countries they serve', and that the two Secretaries General have signed a memorandum of understanding outlining areas of co-operation. In many ways, with their work on election monitoring and embedding democracy, a partnership like this makes sense. But when I asked the Commonwealth for further details – what's in the deal, for example – they simply refused to answer, telling me instead that 'the Commonwealth and the Club de Madrid are currently discussing activities to deliver under this MoU. Until those details are finalised, we will be unable to provide any further information on this matter.' And then there's this. If you look carefully at the press release announcing the agreement, you'll see that the Club of Madrid is still calling itself 'the World Leadership Alliance-Club de Madrid'. The two have become one; seven years on and the WLA name survives, bringing back happy memories of Coolum Beach in December 2013.

CHAPTER 3

THE CAMPAIGNER

In a cream-coloured photo album on my bookshelf, amongst pictures of friends, trips around the US and basketball games, there's a photo of me, dressed in a dark blue velvet jacket, shaking hands with former US President Gerald Ford. I have mixed feelings when I look at it: a slight squirm because of the jacket, but also pleasure because it marks the point, in the spring of 1999, at which I became interested in the power and possibility of a former President to change the national conversation. Ford had come to my university as a visiting lecturer, to speak about leadership and about the difficult decisions he had made in office, and about his life afterwards. I remember the excitement of meeting my first President (albeit a former one), and I remember the story his former adviser, and my professor, David Gergen told about underestimating Ford as he tried to carve out a post-presidential career for himself. But above all I remember the op-ed Ford had written a few weeks earlier, at the height of the Clinton impeachment saga. Like the outcome, the politics of the Clinton impeachment twenty years ago weren't all that different from those surrounding President Trump in 2020. The House, controlled by the opposition party, decided that he had committed an impeachable offence, and it was then up to the Senate, controlled by the President's party, to decide whether he should be convicted – and removed from office. The atmosphere, then as now, was poisonous, and many observers were deeply worried about the effect on the nation, a little over twenty years after Richard Nixon resigned rather than be impeached. Into the breach stepped Ford, who having succeeded and then pardoned Nixon knew a thing or two about the politics of impeachment. He was joined by his one-time political foe turned friend and ally – and occasional election-monitoring companion – Jimmy Carter. Together, the two former Presidents penned an article, published in the *New York Times*, entitled 'A Time to Heal Our Nation'.[1] 'However one now supposes a trial may end,' they wrote, 'it seems inevitable that by rehashing the lurid evidence of President Clinton's misconduct, we will only exacerbate the jagged divisions that are tearing at our national fabric.' They reviewed some history from previous impeachments, but this tear in the national fabric is what really concerned them.

> Somehow we must reach a conclusion that most Americans can embrace and that posterity will approve … Our political system, too, is on trial. Can we find within ourselves the will, the vision, the generosity and, yes, the courage to resolve the present crisis in a way that makes Americans proud of their leaders, their institutions and themselves?

In this spirit they offered what they called 'a unique punishment for a unique set of offenses'. They suggested that lawmakers should pass a motion of censure which Clinton, in turn, would accept, acknowledging both his wrongdoing and the harm he caused. The two Presidents' proposal caused a media sensation and, coming both at the height of the saga and just a few days before Christmas, helped frame the conversations millions of American families had during the holiday season. It didn't work out the way they had hoped: the Senate trial continued and in a largely party-line vote Clinton was acquitted. Despite this, it seemed to me then, as now, that this was an interesting use of a former President's ability to if not quite campaign then certainly make an appeal to public opinion. And since then many others have taken a similar course.

•　　•　　•

'I must say to you very candidly that I had no idea of the magnitude of the problem, the complexities of the problem. Now I have been much more informed, and I feel more free to say.' In a wood-panelled room at Chatham House, the former Brazilian President Fernando Henrique Cardoso is talking about how he changed his mind on drug policy. I'm here because Cardoso, along with two other former Presidents from Latin America – the continent most affected by a set of policies known as the war on drugs – has just published a report which is to change the debate about drug policy, not just in Latin America but around the world. 'The other day one friend of mine from Brazil who is a possible candidate in Brazil, he's very close to me, he belongs to my party, he said, "You know people are asking me about your ideas about drugs."'

I hadn't known much about Cardoso before the interview. I'd just started research for this book and trying to understand the backstory of every former Ex Man who passed through London was a bit of a stretch. So I'd ordered his book *The Accidental President* and speed-read it over a couple of days.[2] Thankfully, it's well written and engaging, designed more as a history of modern Brazil than as a detailed policy exposition. What I learned was this: that Cardoso was the first democratically elected President in Brazilian history to serve two complete terms in office, that he was a sociologist before the presidency but because of political repression in Brazil spent many years abroad, that he is a centrist politically, and that he managed to tame inflation and introduce a semblance of order to the Brazilian economy. In other words, he is a boat-righting, rather than a boat-rocking, kind of guy. Drug policy will necessarily be a central concern for any senior political figure in Latin America, and FHC, as he is known, is no exception. But the reason for telling me about his political fellow traveller back in Brazil is to make a point about how the war on drugs has played out there, and not just in the West. 'I remember once, a long time ago, I was a candidate for the mayorship of São Paulo, and my opponent said that I was in favour of marijuana,' FHC tells me.

> At the time I didn't realise the damage this simple suggestion would provoke on my votes, and he did in fact. I had no idea, because personally I had never tried even a cigarette. In spite of that, in the electoral campaign if one side says, 'You are in favour of liberalisation,' this provokes, immediately, tremendous damage.

He pauses. 'So now, I don't care.'

It's this last remark which really captures the importance of what FHC and his fellow Presidents, Ernesto Zedillo from Mexico and César Gaviria from Colombia, have done. Their report, the result of months of work on a civil society project called the Latin American Commission on Drugs and Democracy, upended decades of what politicians in Latin America were supposed to say about drugs. The first words of their final report are 'A Failed War' and after noting that drug-related violence is a growing problem across the continent, they baldly state, 'Prohibitionist policies based on the eradication of production and on the disruption of drug flows as well as on the criminalization of consumption have not yielded the expected results.' The rest continues in that vein, along the way taking shots at both the US, for its one-size-fits-all prohibitionist approach, and reformers in the EU, who in the former Presidents' judgement placed insufficient emphasis on reducing drug use. Ultimately, they suggested a new paradigm: 'Treating drug users as a matter of public health; reducing drug consumption through information, education and prevention; and focusing repression on organized crime', but the headlines came from the positive description of decriminalisation. Viewed from 2020, this sounds like pretty tame stuff; in 2009 it was explosive. So I ask him about that last remark – does he really not care about the political fallout?

Frankly no, because I think it is so important to deal with the subject matter that although it could eventually provoke one or another problem, I think we have to face the question. It is so dramatic what is happening in Latin America, across the world, in terms of drugs, and the amount of money spent in fighting drug users and traffickers is enormous, and my sense is that the governments are missing the war. Even the vocabulary is wrong, it is not a war – it is another thing, so you have to pay attention to the users and say maybe this requires healthcare, not prison, and to concentrate the efforts against the traffickers. And simultaneously it's important to ask attention for those who are using drugs that indirectly they are also giving subsidies to crime. It is a double-fronted battle.

I wonder if this is an atonement, of sorts, for not doing more about this issue when he was in power? 'Well, maybe you're right,' he replies.

I'm not completely sure. When I was in government the problem was violence, and behind violence is drugs, but we were
concerned with violence. And I had not clearly in my mind the
linkage between the violence and the use of drugs. I must say that
maybe in the case of Brazil it is a relatively recent phenomenon,
the widespread use of drugs. I must say that of course when I
became President the problem was already there, but every year
it is becoming more dramatic, so maybe this also motivates me to
be more active.

Whatever the motivation, the report these three Ex Men produced
had an outsize impact. 'It fundamentally changed the debate on
drug policy,' according to Dr John Collins, executive director of the
international drug policy unit at the LSE. 'This is the first time that
you've got former Presidents from a region that has fought the war
on drugs saying the war on drugs is a bad idea. In 2009 that was
huge.' It's not that the Ex Men were the only people saying these
things; far from it. In fact, activists had been making these arguments for years. But never before had credible, establishment figures made these kinds of arguments.

This was three very high-profile figures starting a debate to say,
'Look, the war on drugs hasn't worked, we need to look at alternatives.' Prior to 2009 that would have been read as 'legalise
everything', which would have been seen as too radical. After '09
you start to see this tidal shift in public opinion, which is 'Actually
yeah, the war on drugs hasn't worked that well', 'Maybe we should

consider alternatives', 'It's cost a lot of money', 'Marijuana could be legalised, why do we still have prohibition around it?' All the embryonic arguments start to come to the fore.

It created a bandwagon effect. In Mexico, former President Vicente Fox – Zedillo's successor and, unlike him, a politician from the centre-right – soon backed the recommendations (he has since become an outspoken advocate for marijuana legalisation and is working with a company to bring cannabis to market across Latin America). Elite opinion in Latin America began to change, as then Vice-President Joe Biden discovered when he visited the continent. 'He encountered Latin American leaders saying, "We think this issue is failing and we're not happy to keep going," and Biden said publicly, "This is a legitimate issue for debate,"' John Collins explains. Years later, there is still a note of incredulity in his voice at this point. 'If you talk to any White House advisers, that would never have been admitted in a previous US administration; that was so radical to anything in the last century of US drug policy. Elite opinion had shifted significantly and the US was willing to acknowledge it as well.' Those who had set up and supported the Latin American Commission (notably George Soros's Open Society Foundations) forged ahead, next setting up the Global Commission on Drug Policy. This took the same approach, blending even newer research with credible establishment figures (the three Latin American pioneers were joined by another tranche of Ex Men) to take the arguments global. This second report 'legitimised debate in a very public, very big way', as Collins puts it, and ultimately prompted the first sitting President, Juan Manuel Santos of Colombia, to back the call for change. There were thousands of press stories the day after that report, so the message went far and wide. The next report was backed by a batch of

Nobel laureates and was reported slightly less widely; by 2016 there was dramatically less coverage. To Collins, this was a sign that these arguments were no longer news: by opening the space for people to change their minds, both in policy-making circles and amongst the public, the Ex Men had done their job. Since then, the reform campaign has been much more complicated because it has been more splintered. There is no single, and certainly no simple, policy response. Legalisation or decriminalisation; flexibility within exist-ing treaties or treaty change; treatment or prison for drug users; how to deal with different drugs. Different countries want to try different things at different speeds; some don't want to change at all. Unsur-prisingly, perhaps, as a result the UN has not been able to significantly reform its position. But none of this diminishes the impact or impor-tance of the three Ex Men's achievement. And for at least one of the other Ex Men involved, Ernesto Zedillo of Mexico, who served on both the Latin American and Global Commissions, that was never the point. When I speak to him, in a particularly drab room at the InterAction Council meeting in Wales, he tells me what he expected at the very beginning.

> When I get involved in any of these international endeavours, I don't do it thinking that we will succeed the next day. I think we must be mindful of historical experience and recognise that change doesn't come that fast. And in my case, I think what is important is to contribute, whatever modestly I can, more to the intellectual discussion of the issues. I'm not good for advocacy at all.

This may sound like a strange remark from a central player, but not if you understand his background. If Cardoso hadn't already used the title *The Accidental President* for his memoirs, Zedillo surely could have nabbed it for his. An intellectual for whom politics was always conducted quietly, behind the scenes, he became a presidential candidate only after his party's first choice was murdered during the campaign. But his description of how he got involved in the first commission reveals the complex, intersecting web of interests and personal connections that ties Ex Men together at this level. 'For me it was very important that President Cardoso and President Gaviria were involved. I have great respect for those two men, and when President Cardoso asked me to be part of it, there was no way that I could say no.' But it was really the spiralling violence in Mexico that formed the backdrop. 'After the first decade of this century, violence started to grow exponentially in Mexico. At that moment I said, "That's it for Mexico" – neither Mexico nor Colombia can continue on the same track because look what's happening.'

• • •

That instinct, to 'look what's happening', was the driving force behind The Elders' campaign on child marriage, too. And it covered some of the same territory as the drugs commission. 'A lot of groups have worked on this for years,' says Margaret Hempel, at the time director of gender, racial and ethnic justice at the Ford Foundation, one of the world's largest philanthropic foundations, leading a team managing millions of dollars in grants on reproductive health and women's rights. 'And then this comes in and gives it a whole different energy, attention and funding.' But unlike the drugs commission, the campaign on child marriage was less about legitimising a debate that had already been taking place and more about turbocharging it. And when Hempel heard that Mabel van Oranje, The Elders' CEO, was interested in this area, she realised this was a huge opportunity for her, for her foundation, and for the millions of young women who had to endure early marriage each year.

> We were redesigning our youth portfolio at the time, and one of the things that Ford often says is that it really focuses on those who are most marginalised. And I started looking at our portfolio and was thinking, 'We don't do anything on this issue.' It had never been an issue that I was that aware of.

There's a long pause and then she says, 'So,' another pause, 'our bad, right?' She laughs, and tells me that while people within Ford had worked on it,

> we'd never stepped back and really looked at 'If we say we're reaching the most marginalised, what do we do about this group of young women who kind of by definition become extremely marginalised when they get married, so much so that they fall off our screen?' They're not in youth programmes, they're not in schools, they're no longer considered youth so they're not going to youth-friendly services.

She asked consultant Margaret Greene to fill her in. Greene by this time was already doing some work for The Elders, and she eagerly shared her data with Hempel; in turn, as she read into the subject, Hempel realised this was a potentially game-changing issue. 'As a team we were grappling with how you get people to understand that when you're working with young people it's not an either/or. It's not education or reproductive health services; it's not skills development or community building; you have to do all these things.' Hempel pauses again here before she continues.

And I wish truly people could look at a young woman or a young man and recognise that, but they don't. And so there was something compelling that when you describe the forces that contribute to child marriage and what it takes to prevent that and build a different future for those young women, people get it. So economic development colleagues were like, 'Oh, that makes sense'; I was in the repro team so obviously it made sense; education were like, 'We get it, of course.' So, for us that became very powerful as well, as a way of centring girls' experiences.

Hempel is important in this story for more than just her work at Ford; she brought together other philanthropic foundations to share her thinking and allow all of them to work together on this issue. As they did, this effort ensured there was vital financial backing and institutional support for the kinds of ideas The Elders were beginning to discuss.

Meanwhile, van Oranje was busy establishing a network of organisations already working on the issue who she felt could use The Elders' support, and the foundations' support, and to assure the world that this was an issue with genuine grassroots momentum. This was about creating a different context and a different set of possibilities. The Elders team organised an international meeting in Addis Ababa in the summer of 2011 which brought a lot of local African NGOs together with some of the major global organisations for a very intense, well-structured three-day workshop to discuss creating a global campaign. Mary Robinson was one of those who took part. 'We did invest a lot of real time and energy initially,' she recalls.

I went with Archbishop Tutu and Gro Brundtland to Ethiopia, to the Amhara region. We went out to two villages, where we wanted to show good practices in those villages in dealing with child marriage, that it's a whole-village approach. Listening to them, sitting on benches and being photographed listening to the villagers, the child brides, the girls in front of us who were still at school, then talking about what we'd heard.

Next up was a visit to the Indian state of Bihar, where the same group – plus Indian civil society activist Ela Bhatt – chose a school which was seeking to address child marriage. The group split into two, with Ela Bhatt and Desmond Tutu going to see the boys, and Robinson and Brundtland listening to the girls. Eight years later, and with countless other visits in between, Robinson can still remember what they were told.

What would happen would be a fourteen-year-old girl would hear her parents whispering together and then there would be a meeting in a room she wouldn't be in. She'd tell her friends, 'I think I'm going to be married off.' And they would come round and plead with the parents, 'Please leave her for another year.'

Meanwhile, Bhatt and Tutu were telling the boys to do their bit by not taking child brides; the whole group later spoke to women in local government, whom they encouraged to speak out on this issue. And then they took the stories they had heard and shared them with policymakers. 'It was using our voice and our experience and talking about it and being very upfront about what we had learned and what we had listened to, what the reality was on the ground,' Robinson concludes. But they didn't just talk about it in the abstract: The Elders launched their child marriage initiative. The location they chose couldn't have been more distant from Amhara or Bihar. It was the hottest ticket in global philanthropy, the beating heart of what journalist Matthew Bishop called 'philanthrocapitalism': the Clinton Global Initiative. In front of the world's media and everyone who was anyone in the worlds of philanthropy and development, The Elders launched their campaign. As one insider puts it now, 'That was really when we did the big hit internationally, and it really started to take off after that as an issue.' The world stage was set differently in 2011 than it is today; events like the Clinton Global Initiative and the World Economic Forum felt fresh and exciting, providing platforms for global leaders to be challenged on what they would do about global problems, and to try to answer them.

This, then, was The Elders at full stretch, but it was also, according to van Oranje, a result of some basic, early insights. 'Change ultimately needs to happen on the ground in the lives of the girls, of their families, of the community. And that needs to happen in more than 100 countries. So The Elders cannot single-handedly make that change happen,' she tells me.

But what they can do is create space for those who can actually make that change happen to come together, and empower them to do that. I sometimes compare it to being a bit of an icebreaker. They were the first ship going through the ice, and they created the space for everybody else to come in and to start working on this. We realised this was going to require the United Nations to step in. It was going to require governments to step up, both donor governments in the West and also governments of countries with higher rates of child marriage. It was going to require media to do more. It was going to require religious leaders, traditional leaders, to engage. But ultimately, for real change to happen on the ground, non-governmental organisations, civil society, had to play a crucial role, especially local civil society, groups that are actually trusted by local communities.

So much of this book is about intangibles – how does influence work. But the reason I've dwelt on this case study is because we can see two things happening, quite clearly. First, like the drugs commission, we have a bunch of major international figures saying, 'This is a big, important issue, please take note.' Their ability to attract the media spotlight was important. Second, creating this global campaign, which eventually spun out as a separate organisation, Girls Not Brides, was tangible. They created a completely new global partnership which has effected changes to the legal framework, to budgets and to the conversations around this issue at the highest levels, both nationally and internationally. But this issue also needed something which the drugs commission didn't: money. 'If you're doing strategic grant-making and you believe that public opinion and narrative and leadership matter, you pay attention,' Margaret Hempel says with a smile.

> You think about how to help mobilise from that. I think for our leadership, because at the time philanthropy in general was thinking about where can philanthropy lend its voice, seeing The Elders step up so publicly, so visibly and so passionately on this created a space for others to say, 'Yes we stand with them.'

The choice of Elders to lead – Desmond Tutu, Graça Machel, Ela Bhatt, Mary Robinson and Gro Harlem Brundtland – was also significant, according to Hempel.

> It was brilliant because that made it truly a global conversation.

And I really do think it lent a small 'm' moral authority. Those of us working in this space hadn't seen that before. And because their message was about human rights, because it was the leadership from two African leaders, it was about more than just stopping marriage: it really was about what kind of future do we want for girls.

At the end of our conversation about how this campaign had such an impact, Hempel and I have a long discussion about how important The Elders were in creating this change, and how important this issue was for them. In other words, could someone else, or some other group, have done it? Conversely, perhaps this was the only such issue available, and The Elders' success is less a reflection of the possibility for Ex Men to effect change and more a result of Mabel van Oranje's diligent hunt for an issue? During that discussion, Hempel makes three points which I think are really important. First is that the campaign against child marriage, unlike many issues, didn't challenge corporate interests. Second, this is something which seemed possible: 'The genius in early awareness-raising around it – and I don't know if it was conscious on behalf of Mabel and some of the other people – is that this is an issue where it's possible to imagine a significant change in less than a lifetime,' she tells me. And third, in learning from this episode she thinks it's important to ask the right question.

So it may be more a question of not 'Would powerful voices stepping in and framing an issue make a difference?' but 'How would they step in?' What is the frame and the authority that they would bring behind those messages? And that may need to look very different than what was possible ten years ago.

The Elders' strategic decision to establish Girls Not Brides as a separate NGO with a mandate to coordinate across civil society, and to bridge the divide between funders, international NGOs and civil society in Africa, Asia and Latin America, demonstrates a shrewd understanding of the limits to which Ex Men can communicate with, and persuade, the general public. On the other hand, their work at global political level on this issue, or at regional level on drug reform, shows that they very much can shift elite opinion. But remember Ernesto Zedillo's remark? 'I don't do it thinking that we will succeed the next day ... I think what is important is to contribute, whatever modestly I can, more to the intellectual discussion of the issues.' Zedillo has, since very shortly after he left office, had a base at Yale University, where he now runs the Center for the Study of Globalization. From that perch, he has contributed to numerous blue riband commissions – as well as both the drugs commissions, there was the Global Commission on Elections, Democracy and Security, the Global Development Network, the Regional Migration Study Group and the High-Level Commission on Modernization of World Bank Group Governance. He has written and published about drug policy and about globalisation. This is campaigning of a different variety altogether.

• • •

There's no point lying to you that losing political office is a lot of fun; it's not. When I write the short story about this one day, it will be entitled 'And when the phone stops ringing...' But it's a really important point of reflection, because then you have to think afresh.

Former Australian Prime Minister Kevin Rudd is typically forthright as he discusses the pain of losing office – in his case twice. But he's also typically lucid in explaining how he thought about what to do next.

> Whatever you choose to do in public life, it's got to be consistent with the values you have to start with, and you've got to be clear-cut about what's important for you in terms of the future, whether it's of the country or the world at large. That should not change either before you get into office, while you're in office or once you leave office. I think if you find yourself bereft at the point at which you leave office, that can often be a reflection that you weren't clear on why you went in in the first place. The reason I say that is that politics is just one mechanism through which you can advance your values, and the reform agenda that you're committed to. There are multiple other mechanisms as well.

Rudd tells me he's always been very clear about what he wants to achieve but also, since leaving office, clear about what variety of mechanism is not for him. 'You have to think afresh, "Am I primarily interested in the professed policy passions because of my ability to deliver change, or am I primarily interested in them in order to be the centre of attention?" If it's the latter, there's a strong ethical case for getting out of business as early as possible,' he says wryly.

> If it's the former ... then it doesn't take a whole lot of intellectual effort after your political effort comes to a close to work out how you can contribute. You can write, you can speak, you can go to universities and lecture, you can go and head think tanks, you can research, you can set up foundations. You can become a direct actor yourself through those foundations.

Rudd has a portfolio career these days which encompasses all of these routes. He's speaking to me from the Asia Society Policy Institute in New York City, where he's been president since 2015. Described as a 'think-do tank', it seems to have been set up to attract Rudd, a fluent Mandarin speaker whose long-term interests include the question of how to integrate China into the global order without compromising global values. It's not hard to see the attraction: at fifty-nine (when I am speaking to him in 2016), he is loquacious, intelligent and politically savvy. And as he continues, it's his reflections on the value of political savvy which most interest me. 'Through multiple incarnations you pick up different boxes of expertise, different boxes of insight, different boxes of knowledge about how to get things done. And that I think leaves you in a position where you can add value in a post-political career if that's what you choose to do,' he says. This is the argument I heard expressed at the GLF meetings, but it's layered in his case with this think tank job – being paid to take a longer-term view; given the privilege of time.

> If you are able to think your way through a hard problem, and then you're able to interpolate that thinking into the deliberations of government, either your own or those around the world, and they take it up and run with it and they succeed, it's a very satisfying thing to see results delivered. You can usually measure the level of effectiveness by the level of, shall I say, quietude you adopt for your own role.

He laughs again. 'So if you're able to give political leaders some ideas about how to solve a problem, it's a good thing. I've been trying to do that the last couple of years.' This is the premise of the GLF, of which Rudd is a member, and I suspect he's right about the quietude. But that laugh! Kevin Rudd may be loquacious, intelligent and politically savvy; but he's also very ambitious, widely believed to covet the job of UN Secretary General, and hasn't always been known for his quietude. So it's complicated.

Meanwhile, on the other side of the Atlantic, at King's College London, Kevin Rudd's one-time deputy has also found a home inside an academic institution. Julia Gillard was both Rudd's successor and his predecessor, Australia's brutal political culture enabling them to vent their frustrations and get their revenge through the time-honoured tradition of a leadership challenge. These days Gillard talks about her 'post-political' life and wears a number of hats, running organisations involved in global education and mental health as well as her role at King's, where she chairs the Global Institute for Women's Leadership. And in one of her first speeches here, also in late 2016, she gives glimpses of why such an appointment would be valuable. In a speech which blends some of her own story with that of the Commonwealth and some questions around nationalism and identity, she talks about the convening power of educational institutions to focus attention on countering extremism. She's thoughtful if a little dry; but it's in answering questions that the value of her realpolitik, of having someone at this institution who has actually served at the highest level, becomes clear. In answer to a question from a British Member of Parliament about whether Sri Lanka should be expelled from the Commonwealth for its treatment of its Tamil minority, Gillard simply asks why that would be a better solution than engagement. 'There is more frankness in the leader-only discussions than the view from the outside might lead people to believe,' she says. She answers other questions in a similarly forthright way, and stays on afterwards for dozens of selfies and to speak to everyone who so wishes; the event's chair jokes that the reason the Q&A lasts so long is because she is actually answering questions. But it's her description of the Commonwealth as a potential 'thought leader' that stays with me. She may or may not be right about that, but in finding new avenues for sharing her experiences and ideas, she and Rudd are, finally, on the same path again.

• • •

Appointments at think tanks (or 'think-do tanks') and policy institutes give these Ex Men opportunities to influence public life through the power of their ideas, and through their ability to deliver them in a way which academics or thinkers who haven't ever been responsible for delivering policy change might struggle with. But there is another route of influence. It was on Kevin Rudd's list, and every single Ex Man I've spoken to has raised it with me – and that is speaking to young people. Gillard, of course, has chosen to base herself at King's College in London, Zedillo at Yale, and many others take time to speak, visit or base themselves at universities around the world. The African Presidential Studies Center at Boston University even went through a phase of having a president-in-residence; Brown University, fifty miles or so further south, has had a succession of former Presidents either in residence or, like Fernando Henrique Cardoso, as professors-at-large. For the Ex Men, it's an opportunity to share their experience, spread their ideas and perhaps inspire a new generation.

'The bane of development is bad leadership on the continent. In terms of natural resources and people it has everything, but it doesn't take much to see that it's leadership that has been the trouble.' John Kufuor, the former President of Ghana, is a man much in demand

– whether it's as a UN Special Envoy, as a mediator for the African Union or as an election observer for the Commonwealth. He tells me that after eight years as President, he had seen enough to know what he wanted to prioritise during his post-presidential years. 'The first thing that I wanted to do after I stepped down was to launch an inter-generational dialogue with the youth of the country – and hopefully of Africa – on the very, very crucial importance of leadership for all our aspirations,' he answers. Just as I was sceptical of what this meant at the InterAction Council in Wales, I am sceptical here, too, but it turns out he has a very clear vision. He wants to bring people who have succeeded in different walks of life onto the campuses of Ghana's best universities and give students the chance to learn from them. This conversation is taking place in the summer of 2014, and he tells me he's already brought people from finance, engineering, social services and the media, as well as his fellow Ex Men from Germany and South Africa, and Finance Ministers from Nigeria and South Africa, to speak and to field questions, filling the auditoriums with enormous audiences of up to 3,000 students.

'After a student has had, say, a three- or four-year stint on campus, benefiting from interactions like I'm talking about, that person would leave campus not only with a degree but with a stretched mind that would enable the person to see that leadership does not drop from a tree like ripe fruit,' Kufuor says.

You have to more or less apprentice yourself, work your way with a vision, and you need to know the people and the challenges. So the youth who are aspiring, when they get to see how to go about things, that would be the key, and this is the legacy I want to leave.

This is exactly what Gerald Ford was doing with me more than twenty years ago. That's what the photo captures, and why I started the chapter with this otherwise unremarkable anecdote. And every time I think about my experience, or speak to one of these Ex Men about these types of activity, I'm reminded of the parable of the farmer scattering seed. Some of it falls on hard ground, where it doesn't grow; some on stony ground, where it springs up but soon dies back; some amongst the thorns, where it grows but is choked; and some on rich, fertile soil, where it thrives. The farmer doesn't know which seed will land where, so he just has to hope that if he sows enough, he will get a decent crop.

When I put this image to David Nussbaum of The Elders, it turns out he has two theology degrees and is rather delighted with the comparison. But he thinks it's only the first of three reasons to make the effort to reach out towards young people. The second, he says, is a genuine interest in what they're saying. It's a great way to find out what people think and why they think it, to stay in touch with global public opinion, if such a thing exists. I'm less sure about this – I suspect the types of young people who go along to an event where The Elders might speak already have a pretty clear idea of the kind of world they want to live in, and that more likely than not it's based on the liberal, democratic and global values The Elders espouse. And so the third becomes more important: what Nussbaum calls 'encouraging, catalysing and sometimes challenging the perspectives of younger people'. He tells me about an occasion when several of his members were on stage and on the receiving end of some pointed and forceful advice from a young person. 'And one of The Elders said, "Sorry, I think that's quite wrong, that's the wrong way of looking at it, and here's why, and I hope you change your mind." There was a bit of surprise from the young person.' I should imagine there was, because I've found these types of occasions to contain little challenge. At the One Young World summit in London in October 2019, for example, Mary Robinson and Gro Brundtland were interviewed in front of a large audience of young global leaders by British journalist Jon Snow. He posed some thought-provoking questions, but the tone from the two Elders was relentlessly upbeat and positive, albeit – with these particular Elders – also practical and can-do. I remember thinking at the time that if I were a young activist I'd be inspired, but also that the words have a tendency to turn into a blancmange of good intentions. So when Nussbaum tells me that engaging with young people in this way 'isn't just cuddly conversations to say, "Aren't you lovely", this is about substantive engagement' and brings up that very summit, I'm taken aback. Were we at the same event, I wonder to myself?

> We had an informal session, just in a room with circles of chairs, no table, and two or three Elders and some young people just sitting, and conversations. Talking to the young people afterwards, that was such a pivotal experience for them. So if that's something that can inspire and encourage them to keep going when times get harder, that's also part of The Elders' role.

Phew.

• • •

What I find striking about all these examples is that they are all, really, about changing elite opinion – amongst politicians, journalists and other decision-makers (and future politicians, journalists and other decision-makers). Which is not to say they're not interested in shifting *public* opinion, only that it seems to shift indirectly.

But there are plenty of examples of Ex Men speaking directly to the public, or speaking to both groups at once.

In 2011, an earthquake off the coast of Japan caused a tsunami, which in turn cascaded over the walls of the Fukushima No. 1 nuclear power plant, setting in train a catastrophic series of failures. It was the world's worst nuclear accident since 1986, and in Japan it prompted a bout of soul-searching about the future of nuclear power, which until then had generated a significant portion of the country's energy. Amongst those prompted to rethink their support was former Prime Minister Junichiro Koizumi, who had strongly backed nuclear power during his premiership. Koizumi is an unusual figure in Japanese politics. Charismatic and dashing, with a swept-back mane of hair, he is one of Japan's most popular and longest-serving Prime Ministers. So his rethink was significant, and in the years since the disaster in Fukushima, he has made this his signature policy initiative. He co-founded, with Morihiro Hosokawa, another former PM and a political foe, the Japan Assembly for Nuclear Free Renewable Energy. He has campaigned to raise money for US servicemen who say they contracted radiation sickness while working to clean up after the disaster. In 2016, he sharply criticised his successor and one-time protégé, the current Japanese Prime Minister Shinzo Abe, for claiming that the situation at the power station was under control. 'When I was Prime Minister, I believed what they told me. I believed it was a cheap, safe and clean form of energy,' Koizumi told a press conference. 'I'm now ashamed of myself for believing those lies for so long.'[3] In 2018, he published a book on the subject, and he now says it is 'a lie' to claim that nuclear power is 'safe, low-cost and clean', although that was indeed exactly what he once said. It's clear that he is setting out to achieve change not just by trying to persuade his successor to ask questions when his civil servants tell him everything is fine; nor through his son, an up-and-coming political star in Japanese politics; nor even by working with opposition parties on the issue; but to change public opinion. In an interview with journalist Takashi Arichika to mark the book's publication, he said he felt he had been deceived, and that he is working to rectify his past mistakes. 'I did some soul-searching and decided I ought to spread the word that Japan can do without nuclear plants … I am touring across Japan as I am keen to share my thoughts with many people.'4

The trouble with trying to assess what Koizumi and his fellow Japanese Ex Men are doing is that it's almost impossible to tell whether they've made any difference. Like the parable of the farmer and the seed, he just has to put it out there and hope that it lands on fertile soil. But if contributions like these are hard to evaluate, in the UK there's a more cautionary tale about an Ex Man's power to persuade: the tale of Tony Blair and John Major – and Brexit.

Major was Prime Minister between 1990 and 1997. It was not a happy time: his memoir oozes with misery as his increasingly Euro-sceptic party turned on him over Europe. As his majority dwindled, he found it increasingly hard to pass significant legislation; hobbled at home, he appeared ever smaller on the world stage; his relief on leaving office and heading immediately to Lord's cricket ground to watch a match was palpable.5 The contrast with Tony Blair, Major's opponent for much of his premiership, could not have been starker. Blair's ease at their twice-weekly House of Commons outings for Prime Minister's Questions, and his brutally effective press oper-ation, contributed to Major's isolation and misery. In turn, Major authorised a set of advertisements which attacked the Labour leader in particularly personal terms; in British political folklore the posters are known as the 'demon eyes' campaign. It's fair to say

that these Ex Men were not on the best terms. And so pictures of
them side by side, cheerfully chatting away as they walked over the
Peace Bridge in Londonderry, came as something of a shock, even
if it was almost twenty years later. 'It would throw all the pieces
of the constitutional jigsaw up into the air again,' warned Major
at the accompanying press conference of the dangers of voting for
Brexit, 'and no one could be certain where they would land.' The
two former Prime Ministers told the assembled hacks that a vote for
Brexit could 'jeopardise the unity' of the UK, with Scotland perhaps
voting to leave, while in Northern Ireland it risked 'destabilising the
complicated and multi-layered constitutional settlement that un-
derpins the present stability'. These Ex Men were two of the archi-
tects of the Northern Ireland peace process – one getting it started,
the other seeing it through, both putting enormous time and effort
into it – so to hear them warning that 'the unity of the UK itself is on
the ballot paper' was striking indeed. It was all the more so coming
from John Major. Where Blair had been active and visible since the
day he left office, Major had adopted a far stricter diet of media appearances. This always seemed to me a successful effort to maximise
his 'power to persuade': because he intervened rarely, when he did,
his words carried greater weight, and got a bigger platform. I can't
count the times, working for a variety of BBC programmes, I have
had interview requests rejected only to find him pop up at a time
and on a subject of his choosing, and always on a primetime show.
Managing his appearances in this way meant editors were anxious
to have him when offered. I'm sure this was part of the thinking
behind his joint appearance with Blair on that bridge in June 2016.
History doesn't record how many minds they changed, although
Northern Ireland and Scotland both voted to remain in the European Union; it does record that their side lost the referendum. It

also isn't too hard to trace a decline in John Major's effectiveness as a public advocate to this moment. "'Trashing their reputations": Fury as Blair and Major claim Brexit would destroy "UK unity"' was the headline in the *Daily Express*.[6] And while that's exactly the headline you'd expect to find in the *Daily Express*, that sentiment deepened and broadened as Major continued, after the Brexit vote, to advocate first for a so-called soft Brexit, then in favour of various parliamentary manoeuvrings to slow or frustrate it, then in court, and ultimately against his own party and Prime Minister in the 2019 general election. Which isn't to say that Major's involvement wasn't well received in some quarters; just that he became a regular, and predictable, contributor to the political debate, and I suspect his future interventions might carry that little bit less weight as a result.

Meanwhile, the only other living former Prime Minister to get involved in the great Brexit debate, Gordon Brown, came out of it rather better, perhaps because he didn't make it the centrepiece of what he was doing. Indeed, his career as an Ex Man, at least in the UK, could have been modelled on pre-Brexit John Major's: rare interventions on few issues about which he cared a lot. The most notable came during the 2014 Scottish independence referendum campaign, when Brown, a unionist, brokered a dramatic, last-minute commitment to hand further powers to the Scottish Parliament in the event of a 'No' vote. The promise, made by Brown along with his successor as Prime Minister David Cameron and the leaders of the other two major UK political parties, appeared just two days before the vote on the front page of Scotland's *Daily Record* newspaper. Many observers believed it ensured a win for 'No' in the referendum. Three years later, in a video announcing his decision to join the Jewish Labour Movement and urging his colleagues to do the same, and speaking directly to the camera, he told anyone prepared to listen that 'tackling antisemitism and racism and fighting for equality is not a diversion, not a distraction from our purpose as a party, it is our purpose as a party. We will never allow evil to triumph over good, and neither will the British people.' Those words, delivered at the height of the Labour Party's turmoil over how to deal with antisemitism, pinned the most recent Labour Prime Minister's colours firmly to the mast, delivered a rallying cry for all those appalled at the failure to act appropriately, and delivered a scathing assessment of its current leader. And then, in 2020, he was at it again, marshalling a group of the global great and good to co-sign an open letter calling for 'immediate, internationally coordinated action – within the next few days – to address our deepening global health and economic crises caused by Covid-19'. In an echo of his activism and energy as Prime Minister during the financial crisis, Brown was again hitting the phones, calling his friends, fellow policymakers, and his fellow Ex Men. Careful not to be too critical of individual countries or politicians, including British Prime Minister Boris Johnson, he was nevertheless keen to share the lessons of his success during the financial crisis. 'I think the lesson is that, if it's necessary and it has to be done, you have got to work really hard,' he told Isaac Chotiner of the *New Yorker*.[7] In other media appearances he seemed barely able to contain his astonishment at the lack of a coordinated global response. When journalist Gaby Hinsliff at one point asked him whether he felt frustrated not to have the power to do it himself, she recorded, 'A burst of laughter, which I suspect disguises a yes, rolls down the line. "I've got a few ideas that might be able to be helpful, but I'm not claiming anything else."'[8] International co-operation on Covid-19 and the economic recovery may well turn out to be a long-term project, but it is education that has been the central issue of his career as an

Ex Man thus far; an issue which has consumed the vast majority of his time, intellectual effort and political capital since leaving 10 Downing Street.

• • •

In their book *The Strange Rebirth of Labour England*, journalists Francis Beckett and Mark Seddon quote former UN Secretary General Ban Ki-moon describing Gordon Brown as 'the most effective envoy' he had ever appointed.[9] Having worked for both men, Seddon should know, and when we speak on the phone he explains why Brown was appointed to the rather grand-sounding position of United Nations Special Envoy for Global Education. It was far from Brown's first encounter with development questions. As Chancellor, he had been intimately involved in the campaign for debt relief leading up to the 2005 Gleneagles G8 meeting; as Prime Minister, he became increasingly interested in questions of global education policy, as those close to the issue attest. Out of that interest, and the desire to get things done, came the UN appointment. Brown can think on the big stage, Seddon tells me, in addition to which 'he's a grafter, an extremely hard-working details person'. The details which needed the hard graft were how to improve educational opportunities for millions of children around the world languishing in under-resourced schools. Brown's task was to come up with a plan for how to do so. And so the UN set up a commission, the snappily titled International Commission on Financing Global Education Opportunity, to investigate. Brown was to chair it, with an all-star cast of commissioners representing the different constituencies engaged in global education opportunity. Brown's commission beavered away and in due course came up with a detailed plan of action. After which, as Seddon tells it, Brown set to work persuading every conceivable stakeholder in global education policy that this was a good plan and they should back it, which is mostly what has happened. Everyone I've discussed this with agrees that Brown has been an extremely effective advocate for his proposals, using his finance, development and education policy networks, and his ability as a former Prime Minister to pick up the phone and call people he knows. He's persuaded the World Bank and regional development banks, major donor countries like the United Kingdom and Norway, and other key players in global education policy to back his approach. And what of that approach? It's an impressive piece of work. Weighing in at 173 pages, it includes detailed modelling on the number of children likely to be in the education system by 2030, the number of schools and teachers needed to teach them properly, how much they will cost, and how that might be paid for. It touches on teaching methods, technology, inclusion and the need for a different type of education for new jobs. Its central conclusion is that an additional $1.8 *trillion* each year will be needed in low- and middle-income countries, in just ten years. It's a staggering sum, but the report makes a cogent moral and economic case as to why education should be a priority, and proposes some solutions, in particular an innovative new financing mechanism called the International Finance Facility for Education (IFFEd), to help fund it. But not everyone in global education policy is pleased by Gordon Brown's recommendations, or his efficiency in rounding up support for them. Far from it, in fact.

When I read the report, three things leapt out. The first is the gap between the size of that requirement – $1.8 trillion, or $1,800 billion – and the IFFEd designed to help fill it, which is $20 billion a year. Where's the rest going to come from, I wondered, and what has the commission got to say about that? The answers are that it's supposed to come from the countries themselves, through general tax revenue, but you'll search the report's 173 pages in vain for anything much about how they're supposed to generate an extra $1,780 billion. The second point is that this money is to be loaned, not given. And the third thing, which skulks out, rather than leaps out, is only really for connoisseurs of Gordon Brown's use of public service agreements (PSAs) when he was Chancellor of the Exchequer. PSAs were agreements between central government and 'delivery departments' to provide a certain amount of money on condition that they focus on certain outcomes. The Health Department would get some money for some initiative or other on condition that they target hospital waiting times, the Home Office got money but had to prioritise reducing re-offending, and the Education Department got more money for schools but would need to target educational performance, and so on. This is conditionality, it's very familiar, and the education commission's report is full of it. In principle there's nothing wrong with it, but the question is who decides, and who monitors, the conditions? No one with whom I discussed my observations would go on the record, because they don't want to upset Brown, now such a powerful figure in global education policy. But they are really concerned about conditionality because unlike the PSAs, where ultimately British voters could (and eventually did) throw out the government responsible, there's no accountability for the organisations lending the money to the world's poorest governments. Why should analysts at the World Bank or regional development banks be the ones deciding what's best for schools in Pakistan or Côte d'Ivoire, they ask. These Brown-sceptics are worried about the money being loaned rather than given, too, and they're worried that these loans will simply add to already heavily indebted countries' burdens. And third, they wonder why the commission had so little to say about how poor countries could raise all that extra money from tax revenue – that extra $1,780 billion. One critic pointed out to me that if Brown had put as much effort into supporting these countries to broaden their tax bases, improve their tax yields and stop tax avoidance as he has into building support for IFFEd, the sums raised could be much larger, and much more sustainable. None of which is to say that the critics are right and Gordon Brown is wrong. But it is a story with a different ending: of an Ex Man who everyone agrees is being very effective indeed, and of those who really rather wish he wasn't.

CHAPTER 4

THE SPECIALIST

A few years ago, I called up a former British Cabinet minister to ask him some questions about his time in office. I told him I wanted to make a documentary for BBC Radio about his legacy as a minister. There was no guarantee it would be commissioned, I added, but if he was prepared to talk to me, I was very interested in exploring it. He was surprised, and if you know anything about British politics you might be too, for David Clark is hardly a household name. Twenty years ago he served a little more than fourteen months as Minister for the Cabinet Office and Chancellor of the Duchy of Lancaster, a mouthful of a title which, in the way of such things, serves only to exaggerate how unimportant the role is. Why, then, did I call him up? I was – and remain – interested in Clark's example because it seemed to me that what he did better than almost anyone else I can think of is make use of the political capital he had by betting it all on a single project.

When Clark's Labour Party was in opposition, its senior spokespeople (the shadow Cabinet) were elected by backbench MPs. Tony Blair, the leader, didn't get to choose the members of his team, only what jobs to give them. So when his party was finally elected into government, after eighteen long years on the opposition benches, Blair felt obliged to bring the same team with him, even if they wouldn't all have been his first choices. So far, so good; this was also true of several other long-serving party stalwarts from a previous generation of MPs who perhaps wouldn't otherwise have been chosen by the new Prime Minister. But from Day 1 in government, it was clear to most observers that Clark and the other stalwarts wouldn't last long in their jobs: theirs were 'legacy' appointments and the clock was already ticking on their time in office.

When he entered Cabinet for the first time, David Clark was fifty-seven years old. He had first been elected to Parliament twenty-seven years earlier, but because he'd lost his seat during the one intervening period of Labour government, his many years as a party spokesman had always been on the opposition benches, and never in government. So when the opportunity came, the temptation to get distracted must have been enormous. Minister for the Cabinet Office and Chancellor of the Duchy of Lancaster is a something and nothing job – there were a couple of specific responsibilities, but it's a role Prime Ministers usually fill either with someone they want to be a roving problem solver or with a problem they don't want to see rove. Had he wished, Clark could have involved himself on numerous Cabinet committees, spent time reading and commenting on Cabinet papers, representing the departmental position or trying to sway government policy on this or that issue or personal fixation. Many if not most ministers adopt some version of that strategy, either choosing it willingly or simply falling into it, and most of them achieve nothing of note. But Clark chose another route, a harder one for sure: delegating all that work to his deputy and instead focusing his political energy, and what political capital he had, on one or two issues to see if he could make proper progress. And looking through the Labour manifesto, he alighted on one policy commitment which fell firmly within his ambit: 'We are pledged to a Freedom of Information Act, leading to more open government.'

Over the next seven months, Clark busied himself working on a White Paper – a statement of government policy and a precursor to introducing legislation – on Freedom of Information. The result was a maximalist interpretation of that rather slender manifesto commitment – suggesting an ambitious law which would have cracked open the traditionally secretive British state in a dramatic way. Clark focused almost all his energies on this (although he also had an interest in using technology to help modernise government). And I think of him and his team in this period as a little like Frodo in J. R. R. Tolkien's *Lord of the Rings*, eagerly beavering away while trying not to attract the attention of Sauron's eye. For these purposes, Sauron's eye was the Prime Minister's office in No. 10, which was focused on the state of the economy, on Britain's creaking public infrastructure, on rebuilding a relationship with the European Union – on many things, in fact, and certainly not a half-sentence in the manifesto on Freedom of Information. So Clark's White Paper, when it was published, arrived like a thunderbolt. First came efforts to dump as many of Clark's positions as possible; six months later, Clark himself was dumped out of government, and responsibility for Freedom of Information was transferred to the Home Office, amongst the most consistently hostile organs of the British state to the principle of open government. But none of that was enough. Clark's White Paper was out there, and it acted like a very high starting price in a negotiation: it anchored the discussion. Some of its components were watered down, but eventually the Freedom of Information Act passed into law and since it came into force in 2005 has both been a bedrock of investigative journalism and fundamentally altered the relationship between government and the public it exists to serve.

Blair, meanwhile, came to see it as a huge mistake. 'You idiot. You naïve, foolish, irresponsible nincompoop,' he writes of himself in his memoirs. 'There is really no description of stupidity, no matter how vivid, that is adequate. I quake at the imbecility of it.'[1]

Clark's example has been in my mind a lot over the past ten years. Not because I made a documentary about him – as with so many others, it was never commissioned. But because as I've spent time with the various Ex Men I've spoken to for this book, as I read the papers and watch the news and as I receive regular news alerts about the activities of various former Presidents and Prime Ministers, I'm struck by how few Ex Men have followed his example. How many instead follow the other model: the equivalent of receiving government papers and investing time and energy in commenting on them, rather than in trying to be agents of change. Not everyone, of course. This book is full of people who have achieved things in their period after office; the whole point of it is that there are different ways of achieving change, and people have different conceptions both of the appropriate role of an Ex Man and of what is possible. But I am interested in the idea of focus, and one Ex Man I spoke to is a particularly intriguing example of adopting an intense focus on a small number of issues.

• • •

I don't think you should be seeking influence for influence's sake, or to keep your name in the paper, or to have something to do between golf games. It seems to me that you either feel very strongly about the thing that you want to get done or you don't. And then if you feel strongly about wanting to get things done, what you're going to do is go and be involved in those areas, those groupings, where people are doing what it is you want to do. I mean, I go to those IMF meetings because we're in a financial crisis, there are a lot of people there who are working on things and they ask me, 'Would you come? We would like to have your views.'

I'm in a hotel suite overlooking Hyde Park in central London. It's late afternoon in October 2010 and the man I'm speaking to, former Canadian Prime Minister Paul Martin, is in London to address the CBI – the organisation that represents most of Britain's large businesses – but the rumours doing the rounds are that he's really here to advise senior government ministers about how to deal with the impact of the financial crisis on the UK's budget deficit. As Canada's Finance Minister in the 1990s, Martin was instrumental in tackling his country's large and persistent deficit, and in the wake of the financial crisis he's now much sought-after amongst other Western democracies who want to understand how he did it. Martin's approach in Canada involved drastic early cuts to balance the budget, and any sense that the newly elected UK government is minded to try something similar would be politically explosive. I feel slightly guilty, though, because Martin has remained tight-lipped about all that, and so while my fellow journalists have been trying to track him down to substantiate those rumours, and find out what advice he's been giving the UK government, he's sitting with me in a plush hotel suite for a long-planned conversation about priorities. Which at least feels appropriate.

'When you're in government, you have to do a multitude of issues, and there are a multitude of issues that you, directly or through others, can influence or change the course of. And so, because you've got that much greater scope to do things, you take on many more issues,' Martin tells me.

When you're out of government it certainly struck me that you would narrow the focus, because if what you tried to do was to simply accomplish a grocery list, then you'd accomplish nothing. So far better to pick those issues that you feel very strongly about, and certainly in my case issues where I felt that the political capital that I'd built up could really be put to good use, as opposed to issues where everybody was on side. I think the use of political capital to garner public opinion or to push it further on issues where there is not perhaps the same degree of public support or knowledge is very important.

Overlooked issues, in other words, like many of the Ex Men profiled in this book.

By the time I'm speaking to him, the financial crisis has brought him his third prong as a freelance 'budget deficit consultant', but initially Martin chose just two issues for his post-prime ministerial focus. First, working with Canada's indigenous communities on a variety of projects to improve opportunities for young people; and second, chairing a fund to support development in the Congo Basin, in central Africa. But moving from Prime Minister to Ex Man has clearly proved an enormously frustrating experience.

You can do more in five minutes in government than you can do in five months outside of government. That is the justification, in fact, for spending a lot of time trying to get into office. All kinds of people do good, and they spend their whole lives doing good, and sometimes when I was in government I thought, 'Boy, I wish instead of making this speech or going to this place to get into office I could spend all my time doing it.' But there is a trade-off, and that trade-off is that if you spend a lot of time trying to get into office, once you're in office you can do an enormous amount in a very short period of time. And once you leave office, the frustration of not being able to do that – or in my case seeing an extreme right-wing government succeed me and basically turn their backs on things like aboriginal education – was very frustrating.*

Martin was not a wildly successful Prime Minister. A long-serving Finance Minister who over nine years transformed the Canadian economy but enjoyed a tetchy relationship with Prime Minister Jean Chrétien, Martin succeeded to power when support for his party was already slipping away. But he pursued this question of opportunities for indigenous Canadians in and out of office. 'In the case of the treatment of Canada's indigenous peoples, the First Nations, the Métis Nation and the Inuit, the result of 300 years of Canadian history has been a human tragedy,' explains Martin.

> The highest mortality rate, the highest infant mortality rate, the highest incidence of diabetes, Aids, tuberculosis, the lowest incidence of high school graduation. This is an area where because Canada is a rich country, the rest of the world is not going to come to help. They expect Canadians to do it. And there is in Canada, unfortunately, a great deal of indifference to what is human suffering of really epic proportions.

In office, his investment of political capital produced the Kelowna Accord to equalise spending between indigenous and non-indigenous Canadians; out of office it has meant a range of different

---

* The terms 'aboriginal' and 'indigenous' are generally used interchangeably, referring to Canada's First Nations, Métis and Inuit peoples. But the word 'aboriginal' is a government designation, often rejected by indigenous Canadians.

initiatives from education to mentoring in the accounting industry.*
But Martin also wants to use his political capital in sustaining the
public conversation,

> to create a sense of awareness among Canadians so that they
> would realise that governments had to act, and that they had to.
> And I also wanted to use my political capital in order to reach out
> to Canadian educators, to the Canadian business community, to a
> wide range of Canadian leadership to say, 'Look, this is a national
> issue and we can't ignore it.'

I've always assumed that political capital, in these terms, is the
ability to have someone take your call, to speak to decision-makers
about a given issue, to be able to highlight it in the media. And of all
the many Ex Men I've spoken to about political capital over the past
decade, Martin is the most open about what it means, and how he
deploys it. 'It was all of those things,' he tells me,

> but it was also the fact that people tend to be prepared to listen
> – obviously returning calls is part of it – but it's also huge oppor-
> tunities to speak to Canadians and to choose the subject that you
> wanted to speak about. I'd make it very clear when they would
> call me and say, 'We want you to talk about the economy' or 'We
> want you to talk about international affairs' and I'd say, 'Fine, but
> let me tell you I'm also going to speak to you about aboriginal
> issues.'

This, I think, is a very interesting perspective on the public speaking

---

* Paul Martin lost office before he had time to implement the Kelowna Accord, and the
successor government chose not to invest so heavily in indigenous communities.

circuit – being hired to speak to conventions or awards dinners for lawyers or accountants or travel agents – and one I haven't heard before.

> Within the country it is the ability to reach out to people in a way which others who aren't as well known or in the public sphere might not have. It's also the ability, when you start an initiative – and I've started two major initiatives with aboriginal Canadians – that when you say to people, 'I'm doing this, will you help me,' you find they will help you, whether they be the largest companies or whether they be schoolchildren.

Martin mentions a $50 million fund to invest in indigenous enterprises, where twenty major Canadian companies did take his calls and ultimately chipped in; an accountancy mentoring programme for indigenous young people, where he was very quickly able to meet the heads of the big accounting firms who all signed up; and an educational programme which he largely funded himself but where he needed local government buy-in.

> I was able to speak to each of the provincial premiers, just call them and say, 'I'd like to speak to your education ministers,' and they would respond, because they knew this had been a great concern of mine all along. So that ability to reach out to people is certainly part of the political capital.

Martin is emphatic about this latter point – getting through the door is no use unless you've got something to say once you're inside. He clearly believes his years-long investment in the issue helped, but there was more to it than that. 'There's no doubt, as you said earlier, that the ability to make a phone call and have somebody return the phone call, or the ability to make a cold call to somebody you don't know, but who may well have heard of you, is very valuable. But it only goes so far,' he insists.

Unless you have built up a history of experience and knowledge in that area, that experience isn't going to last you very long … But if you call about an area where you're known to have background and knowledge, then yes, very quickly you will be able to engage. That, by the way, is one of the reasons for not doing a grocery list of things when you're out of government, but picking and choosing. You can start off with a certain reputation, but you have to maintain it. I mean if you step down from government and do a Rip Van Winkle [a fictional character who fell asleep for twenty years] for five years and then you came out, your ability to have some influence and do good would be minimal because you'd have lost contact.

It's a point which has been echoed repeatedly in my conversations with Ex Men. When I spoke to former Haitian Prime Minister Michèle Pierre-Louis, for example, she had just returned from a speaking engagement in Washington DC, where State Department specialists had sidled up to her afterwards, keen to hear her thoughts. They weren't interested just because she was a former Prime Minister, though; rather because she was a former Prime Minister who knew what was happening in Haiti right now.

Paul Martin is wealthy from his time before politics, so he hasn't needed to earn money; he hasn't joined any of the clubs; and aside from some issues in which he is just personally interested, he sticks extremely closely to his very narrow diet of causes. That has broadened a little from his original two, but only a little, and as he sits on the sofa in his hotel suite high above London, he seems to me very clear-eyed about what he can – and can't – do.

> The problem is that if I take the three issues on which I'm involved, I'm going flat out. And in fact I can go flat out on the aboriginal issue, I can go flat out on the African issue and I can, unfortunately given the nature of the financial crisis, go flat out on the financial crisis. So on each issue you're taking time away from the other, on those three. So there really isn't the time to be doing other things.

In the ten years since I met him, Paul Martin's engagement with the lives of indigenous Canadians has only deepened. In public, he frequently criticised the Conservative government which succeeded his for failing to properly fund, as he saw it, indigenous schools and education more generally. He's often used paid speeches, and the media access being a former Prime Minister affords, to envision a more equitable, respectful relationship between all Canadians. He worked closely with Joe Clark, a predecessor from the opposite side of the political aisle, on an initiative to promote a new and better relationship between indigenous and non-indigenous Canadians. But in private he's also been beavering away on a variety of schemes to effect change through the Martin Family Initiative (MFI), his private foundation, set up with family money. His deepening engagement sounds a little like unpeeling an onion. It started before I met him, with the Aboriginal Youth Entrepreneurship Program, and ten years on, when I ask Lorne Belmore, the headteacher of one of the first schools to get the programme up and running, what effect it has had, I am startled by his reply. 'I think it's a ray of hope for any school,' he responds. As the headteacher of a successful school serving indigenous students, Belmore had met lots of dignitaries over the years but says he was surprised by Martin's level of engagement. 'Mr Martin's dedication to indigenous causes is above and beyond what I've seen from other people,' he says. 'He was definitely and he still is definitely committed to this programme. It's not so much "Here's a grant: run this programme and write a report". They're very active.' He tells me about the programme: how the details of the course were developed in collaboration with indigenous teachers; how local business people and college professors are brought in to mentor the students and give feedback on their ideas; and how for him becoming an entrepreneur is almost beside the point. He thinks that's Paul Martin's view, too: that this is really about broadening horizons. 'He's not just saying, "Become a businessman, you can make your own money," and walking away,' Belmore says.

> He's committed to saying, 'Here's how we do it, here's what it looks like, here's some money so you can start to see how you control funds.' He's put in steps that are necessary for our people to actually see the steps involved in these sorts of careers that you've never thought of before.

And when I speak to David Richards, Dean of the Business Administration Department at Lakehead University and a mentor with the programme for six years, it's clear that broadening of horizons is part of the plan. For Richards, his involvement with the scheme is partly an opportunity to reach out to potential students in an under-served population and partly because he wanted to work with local high schools. And then he pauses, and laughs. 'I also just thought it would be fun, frankly.'

Lorne Belmore moved jobs a few years ago and feels keenly the lack of the programme in his new school. Because in his years of working with Paul Martin's outfit, he noticed something else about their approach.

> Once you get Martin funding and Martin support, the programme becomes a lot easier to do because they truly do care about what's happening in these classrooms. They're interested in the results, and that makes it very accountable. Exactly what are we doing? How are we making this programme better? How is it affecting our kids? What sort of things can we do to refine it even more?

And this is very much the role the MFI has established for itself – distilling the research to find the best available interventions and then figuring out how best to apply them in real communities. And it seems to me that this is how the onion unpeeling began. Paul Martin started with youth entrepreneurship and accountancy mentoring and an investment fund, because that's what he knew. He and his foundation worked hard to make a success of them. But it rapidly became clear that the challenges facing many indigenous Canadians went far deeper than a lack of business skills or opportunities to mingle with college professors and intern at blue-chip accountancy firms. And over the years, as he and his MFI team have deepened their involvement, they have developed a variety of patches, fixes and solutions. The original schemes have been supplemented by programmes on entrepreneurship for adults, mentorship with law and accountancy firms, financial literacy projects, leadership courses for headteachers and model school literacy programmes. They've all been developed in collaboration with indigenous communities, although Lorne Belmore, an indigenous Canadian himself, tells me that at one stage he was so concerned at the lack of indigenous staff at the MFI that he had a quiet word to emphasise how important it was that it didn't look like 'a white person coming in to fix indigenous problems'.

Martin's journey has culminated in the foundation's newest programme, a scheme which supports young mothers from the start of their pregnancies to the time their children begin school. It's an intensive intervention in the lives of both mothers and children, and it's delivered locally, by workers from their own communities, and designed in collaboration with them. And because it's being delivered by a family foundation, and not government, they're not bound to a single approach, and can both innovate to solve problems as they find them and, occasionally, fail. Government programmes rarely seem able to do either, and by way of example, project director Chloe Ferguson tells me that when the team identified the lack of transportation to get to pre-natal health appointments as a major problem, they fixed it by ensuring everyone working for the programme had access to a vehicle. Ferguson is Paul Martin's former research assistant and speechwriter, and she describes for me the way he and the organisation function.

> Our goal is to work directly with communities in as many cases as possible to identify gaps in service, innovate around what those gaps are and then ensure that communities are adequately supported with government funding to sustain the programmes from a training and content perspective for themselves to run it. So our ethos is very much to work ourselves out of a job.

Of course, as great as these projects sound, none of this matters if they don't work. So how successful have they been? The answer isn't always clear. Anecdotally, the stories are positive – but as a journalist

I'm used to hearing those. The data are less clear, for three reasons. First, some of the projects are really young. Second, the sample sizes are really small. And third, the data belong not to the MFI but to the indigenous communities Paul Martin and his team work with. However, one indication of what's going on is that in almost every case, once MFI has set up, tested and ironed out the initial problems with one of these programmes, other funders have come in behind them. Sometimes that means individuals, companies or foundations; the youth entrepreneurship programme and model school literacy projects are funded by provincial governments; while Canada's federal government is already sufficiently interested in the early years programme to be committing significant funding to it. This time attribution isn't the problem; it's measuring success.

$$\bullet \quad \bullet \quad \bullet$$

At the Global Leadership Foundation meeting in Ireland, it's time for the coffee break as another long session is drawing to its close. I'm only half paying attention as the delegates file out of the main room: some spry, fairly bouncing along; others trudging; but one person stands out. Constantly active, radiating a restless kind of energy, Helen Clark has been fascinating to watch throughout the conference. In the audience, she's always busy – listening, but also reading, writing, typing. Onstage, when someone asks an overlong question you can feel her itching to answer. She listens carefully as she scans the room, feeling its mood, frequently spotting questions before the moderator. In the coffee breaks, she's on the phone, then catching up with her fellow Ex Men, then on Facetime, and just occasionally drinking coffee like the rest of us. No one else at the event is as intense: she feels like a force of nature.

In May 2019, Clark is just over two years on from a failed run to be UN Secretary General; a rare setback for a politician who was a successful three-term Prime Minister of New Zealand before spending eight years as the second most senior official in the UN system, as Administrator of the United Nations Development Programme (UNDP). We've arranged to have a chat during the break, and I'm especially keen to ask her about this specialisation to succeed. As Prime Minister, she had a reputation as a technocrat, figuring out what worked and investing her political capital in doing that. So presumably she has adopted the same approach since leaving office. How has she chosen to invest her time? 'You do have to choose,' she laughs,

> because there's just so many issues. And I tend to range quite widely, because having over the past thirty years stepped up from individual portfolio responsibility to leadership – I mean I first became Deputy Prime Minister of my country thirty years ago – I learned that at leader level you don't want to be bogged down in the details of one issue; you have to have a helicopter view. So I still endeavour to do that.

This, really, is the exact opposite of Paul Martin's narrow focus. 'And what I accept to speak on, be involved in, is generally across the sustainable development spectrum, because I've spent a lot of time on those issues,' she continues.

> But that gets you into so many things, because if you take an overarching view of economic, social and environmental policy there's a lot of avenues you can go down. Obviously, the women's leadership issues. I also continue to keep a profile on both non-communicable diseases and HIV, which I've been very

involved in since I was a health minister in the past. And then I've also picked up the drug policy issues, because I take the view that in general UN conventions are a gold standard of where the world should go, but there's one major exception to that, and it's the drug conventions, which were a disaster and have mandated a prohibitionist approach which has had appalling consequences. So I bat away on that.

By now we've covered large swathes of development politics, from health to environment, and she's still going.

In addition, because I've had a long interest in international affairs, and geopolitics and peace and disarmament, I continue to comment on issues of that kind. So I like to keep quite broadly engaged, but I can't tackle every issue all the time. At the moment I'm tweeting about Libya because the chaos in Libya has been disastrous not only for its own people, but of course for sub-Saharan Africa...

She goes on to talk about Mali and Burkina Faso and Niger and trafficking routes through the Sahel; her whole answer lasts almost exactly three minutes. In other words, she is doing a lot, and I won't lie: I'm surprised. Not only that she's doing it, because the temptation must be incredible, but that she is so resolute about it. No equivocation, no doubt that these are all valuable, or that 'keeping a profile' on one issue might take away time she could usefully invest in something else, something concrete.

Bearing in mind how I started this chapter, it might be tempting to see this as unfocused or undisciplined, but I don't think it is. It's broad, but not unfocused. And a year later, her experience and obvious personal qualities, combined perhaps with this determination to keep across a broad range of issues, mean she's been asked (together with former Liberian President Ellen Johnson Sirleaf) to lead a review into the World Health Organization's handling of the Covid-19 pandemic and, as she tells *The Guardian* in July 2020, to ask, 'What do we need to stop the world being blindsided again by a crisis like this?'[2]

My conversation with Clark echoed, in some ways, a conversation I had in the same small conference room the previous afternoon. The GLF meeting is an intensely international affair. Ex Men, business leaders and representatives of NGOs from around the world have flown in for the occasion. Very few people have driven here, but one of them is John Bruton, who served his country as Taoiseach between 1994 and 1997. Bruton has had a long and at times very interesting post-premiership, including a five-year stint as European Union Ambassador to the United States, and so I'm keen to ask him about this question of achievement, attainment. Which Bruton is immediately keen to downplay: 'One should not exaggerate the power one has as Prime Minister. You do have an agenda-setting power all right, you can prioritise what's going to happen, but on the other hand you don't have complete control.' This is, I'm sure, true. But by the time you leave office, you have even less. 'You're left with influence, either on public opinion or on the people who are in power at the moment, but more so on public opinion,' Bruton agrees. 'At the end of the day, one has to be modest. I mean, nobody is indispensable. And the fact that you're no longer in office doesn't mean that good things cease to happen!' He laughs at this point, and what he says next speaks to a life well lived.

> The important thing is to have a fulfilling life, to try to take an
> interest in the things you find interesting, and do them as much

as possible. Part of the thing I found when I moved from being a spokesman for a particular portfolio in Parliament or being a minister to being party leader was that in the former I could more or less decide what I wanted to do, or what I wanted to talk about, and I would press the things that were interesting to me. As soon as I became party leader I didn't have time to be doing any creative intellectual work. Your job was entirely people management and expectation management, and obviously media appearances, but it was media appearances representing a collective view rather than representing your own creative insight.

He laughs again. 'So one of the upsides in a way of no longer being in a top job is you regain some of the freedom to do the things that really interest you, which of necessity you couldn't indulge to the same degree when you're in the top job.'

With this answer, I feel we're getting to the nub of something. Bruton wants both to do things he finds interesting and to do things which are fulfilling. What can you really achieve, though, if you just focus on things that interest you? He starts to answer, almost spitting out the word 'achieve'. Then he pauses, and when it comes, the answer is slow.

Even as Prime Minister one's achievements are in part the achievements of others, or achievements to which your name is put, even though you may have been only one of the contributors. So I think one shouldn't exaggerate that. But what I think one ought to try to do is to use an event like this to accumulate information which you can then use in speeches or in articles in the paper, things like that. Not to quote them directly but to try to enhance public knowledge of choices that have to be made, or alert the public to things the public, either in your own country or another, ought to know.

'I feel I've done that in respect of Brexit,' he chuckles. As this conversation is taking place, Brexit is at a particularly difficult impasse. The Irish airwaves are full of advertisements telling businesses how to prepare for Brexit, and what it might mean is a source of public conversation. Bruton has been writing regularly in the Irish papers about both, predicting the chaos the process has thrown up.

When others were complacent, I was warning of this. Whether that's an achievement in your terms I don't know, but it's certainly had an impact. One should always try to be having an impact of some kind, rather than just enjoying life. But the two go together: if you're not enjoying it, you won't do it well.

This, then, is how to balance the two: the old adage that if you're doing something you love, it's not really work. In talking about Brexit, Bruton has found new purpose, just as did John Major and Tony Blair. Perhaps, like Paul Martin during the financial crisis, they have simply found their moment to re-engage, found an interested audience and, of course, found an issue that matters. But this focus on a single issue is something I've heard from thoughtful leaders throughout this journey. Not that everyone chooses it, but that with the swirl of invitations and offers, doing one or two things well may be smart. In her office at the Harvard Kennedy School in November 2010, I sit and discuss precisely this question with Michèle Pierre-Louis, the former Haitian Prime Minister. She tells me about the boards on which she sits, and a recent invitation to be part of an international team considering the death penalty. 'I have a lot of invitations to be part of different groups, different organisations,' she continues.

Sometimes I even have to refuse because there are too many. But … I think it would be better for me not to disperse myself, and concentrate on what I can achieve, what is feasible, what is exhilarating in a way. Because it's interesting to see in the chaos that exists in the country that some things are able to be achieved, and that I'm part of it. It's important to me.

CHAPTER 5

THE LEADER

It's June 2016 and the main hall of London's Barbican Centre is packed and buzzing with anticipation. For the first time in its seventy-plus-year history, the United Nations is holding public debates to help decide who will be the next Secretary General. The process won't be truly open, of course; that's not how the UN works. And since this is the second debate in a major Western city – the first was in New York six or so weeks ago – it won't be truly global; that's not how the UN works, either. But at least these cities are true metropolises, and from the sounds and sights tonight it does look as though it's attracted a cosmopolitan crowd. Nobody seems quite sure what to expect. The first debate lacked any big names; this one at least includes the former Portuguese Prime Minister and UN High Commissioner for Refugees António Guterres, alongside lesser-known figures from Montenegro and Serbia, and it doesn't take long for a bit of political naïveté to reveal itself. It's not clear they are serious contenders anyway, but if they are, Igor Lukšić and Vuk Jeremić appear to have forgotten that it will be the five permanent members of the UN Security Council (the so-called P5) who will make the appointment, and not this audience, so playing to this gallery will get them precisely nowhere, especially if it comes at the cost of antagonising the P5. The surprise is Guterres. During a contest in

163

which large parts of civil society are clamouring for a woman to get
the top job, and in a year when someone from Eastern Europe is
supposed to be appointed, this sixty-something man from Western
Europe is storming this room. By my count he gets at least three
vigorous rounds of applause, and interestingly it's not for flights of
fancy but for what sound like rather plodding, practical suggestions:
using his late wife's psychoanalytical framework to bring countries
together by perceiving common interests; ending immunity for
human rights violations committed by UN peacekeepers; and a
description of the steps he took in Portugal and at the UNHCR to
promote women. Unlike his less-experienced opponents, Guterres
manages to do all this without infringing any of the prerogatives, or
even policy preferences, of the P5. He is the evening's clear winner,
and a couple of months later, after multiple rounds of secret voting
inside the Security Council, he is appointed the ninth United Nations Secretary General. He is the first Ex Man to lead the UN, but
the organisation must wait for its first female leader.

• • •

Three years later and the evening before I'm due to interview Helen
Clark, I sit in my room and watch the documentary made about her
failed campaign for the UN's top job. Amid the sense of dejection
when it becomes clear she won't win, filmmaker Gaylene Preston
asks Clark what she'll do next. 'Something constructive to do will be
found,' replies the former Prime Minister. Something constructive
to do will be found! It's such an existential statement: drowning in
bathos and true of almost anyone leaving high office or a meaningful job, but it seems particularly apposite for the ambitious types
this book is about. She can't bear to watch that film, Clark tells me

as we chat the next morning, and I can understand why, but I also can't help asking her about it, and that quote in particular. 'My experience in life has been if you close one door, or if a door closes on you, there's always another one which is open, or can be opened,' she replies. 'My attitude was it's not the end of the world in that contest, because there's plenty of other things to do.'

That certainly seems to have been her attitude eight years earlier, when she lost the 2008 election in New Zealand and stood down as Prime Minister. 'The first thing you do is take a long break,' she laughs.

> In the course of that long break, I stayed with the New Zealand High Commissioner [the country's Ambassador] in London, and he came home one day and said, 'Have you seen that the head of UNDP is stepping down?' and I said, 'Well, actually I did see it.' And he said, 'You should go for that'.

Laughter again, and she relays the debate the two had about the key ingredient necessary to do the job well: was it experience of development, or experience of leadership? One she didn't have, but as the Ambassador pointed out, she had the other in spades. And so at age fifty-eight, Clark prepared her first ever résumé, with a heavy emphasis on her leadership experience and the need for some of it at UNDP. 'My position was that the last thing the UNDP needs is a development professional running it,' she says. 'It's stacked from top to bottom with development professionals, but what it needs is leadership because it's a bit...' and here she pauses, 'out of view at the moment. It's got a good track record, but not that many people know about it. One of my tasks was to make it much more outward facing, and communicate it.' Part of what followed would be recognisable to anyone applying for a job: the résumé, of course; a job interview; a shortlisting process. Some would be less so – the courtesy calls on UN ambassadors, and a final decision taken by someone she already knew: UN Secretary General Ban Ki-moon. 'As Korean Foreign Minister he'd called on me seeking support from New Zealand for his candidacy to be Secretary General.' Did you support him? 'Yes, we did.' Which probably made that subsequent conversation a lot less awkward? 'Yes, and I think Ban Ki-moon was not afraid to appoint people who had held more senior positions in their country than he had held in his. He also appointed Michelle Bachelet, for example, who'd been the President.* He wanted the best for the UN.'

Clark may have campaigned for the job on her leadership record but, as she tells it, once in post she found her whole political life turned out to be useful. Those two years as housing minister, that year in charge of health policy, 'everything I'd ever done in public policy was relevant to UNDP', she says. What's more, because as Prime Minister she had been accustomed to taking a helicopter view of every subject area, 'there was almost no policy issue that came up for UNDP to address in its programming that I didn't know something about'. Transparency became a hallmark of her time at UNDP, an interest which she brought from New Zealand to sit alongside her executive experience. But she brought something else, too: contacts. Whether it was the Commonwealth, the Pacific Islands Forum, the Asia-Pacific Economic Cooperation, East Asia Summit or the many bilateral visits to countries in Latin America, North America, Europe and Asia, after nine years as Prime Minister

---

* Of Chile, from 2006 to 2010, after which she was executive director of UN Women before serving again as President of Chile, from 2014 to 2018. She is now UN High Commissioner for Human Rights.

she had been to a lot of places and met a lot of people. Presumably this meant that when she visited a country in her new job, it was helpful in getting access at the highest level?

> Incredibly helpful, because when you went as UNDP Administrator to countries, UNDP was well positioned in countries. It generally had a good relationship with presidential and prime ministerial offices, planning and finance ministries and so on. If you bring in then a leader who has been head of government, that is the entry point to actually call on the President, call on the Prime Minister.

I've heard this repeatedly from Ex Men: the importance of your network, using the personal connections to your peers and contemporaries. Kim Campbell told me right at the beginning of the process that the network is extremely important and had been a significant factor as she sought to get the Club of Madrid up and running and broaden its membership. But of course it assumes a different character altogether when the Ex Man concerned holds office in a major international organisation and is able to use those friendships with serving leaders to circumvent sclerotic bureaucracies, slothful processes or simply obstructive private offices.

• • •

'We certainly recognised the office was going to be given a real injection of profile and contacts and standing that it didn't have previously.' Scott Jerbi can remember the sense amongst members of staff that things were going to change when Mary Robinson was appointed UN High Commissioner for Human Rights. In the early days he wasn't close enough to see her use her network regularly, but by the end it was clear to everyone what was happening. And one name in particular sticks out: Nelson Mandela. 'He was the first world leader that she turned to, to get other leaders to sign on,' Jerbi recalls. Robinson was trying to drum up support for a statement ahead of the 2001 World Conference Against Racism, and she went straight to the man with the biggest moral sway, whom she knew from her time as Irish President. 'That's not something typically that anyone other than a UN Secretary General would do. The pecking order would be that the Secretary General is the one engaging with heads of state, and Under-Secretaries General – her level – wouldn't do that too often.' But Robinson's history as a human rights advocate of long standing and a former head of state was, he says, 'perceived as raising the profile and the legitimacy and the importance of the office within the UN system and on the world stage'. But if it took a couple of years to call on Mandela, it was clear right from the beginning that she would speak up on the job in a way that her pre-decessor had not, and that she had, according to Jerbi, 'a presence, and a personality, and a name that was already well known'.

It's striking if you look at Mary Robinson's record, and particular-ly if you read her memoir, where she very consciously draws out the strands connecting the different periods in her life, how similar the structural challenges facing her in the two jobs were.[1] As President of Ireland, she had campaigned to make more of the role, to speak up for the people who had elected her. She used the symbolism of the presidency, her own moral standing and political independence and a very deliberate and careful reading of her constitutional man-date to push back against political efforts to restrict her freedom of manoeuvre. Jerbi suggests I look again at the UN General Assembly Resolution 48-141, which created the office of High Commissioner, to see that it's a strange hybrid. 'It is designed to be a public promotional voice, but it also does have practical and real responsibilities within the system that are beyond just being an advocate,' he tells me. Successful politicians often take mandates like these and stretch them to suit their political ends. I'm reminded of how Ken Livingstone, the first directly elected Mayor of London, made maximum use of the extremely limited formal powers handed to him to bully, cajole and – that word again from Richard Neustadt – persuade others to do his bidding. And when I asked Mary Robinson about the similarities in her approach as President and High Commissioner, she agrees.

> That was where I learned how to try to use the moral voice and the pulpit that I had on behalf of the people of Ireland. I think I must be a mandate person – I hadn't reflected on it before – but I took 100 per cent seriously the inaugural address that I gave.

Robinson was helped at the time by Kofi Annan, then UN Secretary General, who wanted to 'mainstream human rights', by which he meant include it as a consideration in every programme, in everything the UN did, rather than confine it to a silo. And for someone with that agenda, Robinson's appointment was a powerful signal, to civil society and particularly to the big human rights organisations like Amnesty and Human Rights Watch, that he was serious. Not only did Robinson have a lifetime working on human rights cases in Ireland behind her – as an activist, lawyer and politician – but as President of Ireland she'd visited Somalia amid its famine and Rwanda after its genocide, to do what she could to focus not just Irish but world attention on the challenges.[2] But if civil society was delighted with the appointment and her willingness to speak out in public, over time some governments would be rather less so. Within the UN system she pressed to achieve the bureaucratic part of her mandate; reorganising, expanding and funding the office, and making the case for human rights more broadly. It's something she was clearly less comfortable with and a tremendous challenge for someone with no previous experience of the UN. That her successor was more street-savvy at navigating that labyrinthine bureaucracy – having what Scott Jerbi calls 'a more operational profile' – perhaps indicates that she'd done her part to establish the office and make the case for it; now it was time to bed it in.

· · ·

'The reason why I was asked to become Secretary General of NATO was a general strong wish among heads of state and government within NATO to carry out profound reforms of the organisation.' Anders Fogh Rasmussen was, from 2009 to 2014, Secretary General of NATO, having stood down as Prime Minister of Denmark to take up the job. 'Of course, I knew beforehand that it would be quite a challenge,' he continues. 'There's a clear difference between being Prime Minister and being Secretary General of an international organisation like NATO. To put it very bluntly, as a Prime Minister, though you can't take all the decisions yourself, you do have instruments to ensure that your political direction will be followed.' He chuckles here before continuing, 'because eventually you can dismiss a minister. But you don't have that as Secretary General of NATO. You can't just ask Chancellor Merkel or President Obama to resign if they do not follow you! So you have only one instrument, and that is the weight of your argument.'

Like the UN, NATO had a reputation for being sclerotic, hard to manage and dominated by the bureaucracy, with the nations' ambassadors having an outsize sway. With the end of the Cold War there was a widespread feeling that NATO had lost its way, and perhaps its role; but by 2009 it seemed newly relevant again. Members felt that new threats, whether from unstable states, international terrorism or a more assertive Russia, needed to be confronted, and the Secretary General would have to lead that process. The problem was, as Karl-Heinz Kamp, a commentator on NATO and at the time I spoke to him the academic director at the German Federal Academy for Security Policy, told me, that too often the men (and they have all been men) appointed Secretary General found the position to be 'less of the general and more of the secretary'. But Rasmussen wasn't afraid to ruffle feathers. He was the first Secretary General directly elected at a NATO Council, and more importantly the first former Prime Minister to run the alliance in more than sixty years, bringing with him a reputation as a reformer.

Rasmussen tells me that he used three instruments to set the agenda. The first of these was speech-making, which he says 'more or less set the direction for NATO and prepared the ground for new initiatives and new directions'. These new initiatives included a new strategic concept to deal with the challenges facing the alliance, a beefed-up rapid reaction force based in Eastern Europe, and six military operations on three continents. Rasmussen says the second core instrument was to use the office of Secretary General to facilitate agreement in the NATO Council – the principal decision-making body, where ambassadors meet weekly but decisions must be consensual, making preparatory work essential. This was often the sticky part of the organisation, where a lack of consensus could block progress. So far, so good; any incoming Secretary General with a strong mandate could, and did, make use of these instruments. The innovation was the third instrument, and could, I suspect, only have come from an Ex Man.

> I always had the ability to call former colleagues among heads of state and government. It was a unique platform for me as former Prime Minister to use that – you might call it a weapon. If it was difficult to achieve consensus at the level of ambassadors or ministers, then they all knew that as last resort I could just take the phone and call President Sarkozy in Paris or Chancellor Merkel in Germany to make sure we moved in the right direction. So these three instruments were my weapons, so to speak, as Secretary General of NATO.

And Rasmussen is unusually candid in talking about the importance of that network of former colleagues still running member countries, both in doing the job and in getting it in the first place. 'I held the rotating EU presidency in the second half of 2002, when we decided the historic enlargement of the European Union. So already from early on during my term as Prime Minister of Denmark, I established a very broad international network, and continued to cultivate that network.'

Karl-Heinz Kamp had told me that going over the heads of ambassadors was a marked change from previous Secretaries General, and that some of the ambassadors deeply resented having their power diluted in this way. I assume, I ask Rasmussen, that he did this to establish that strong leadership at the centre?

> Yes. It was like the nuclear threat. To have that weapon, you can use it, and they know that you can use it as a last resort. And because of that threat, ambassadors usually found a consensus themselves

without having me to actively implement my calls to national heads of state or government. So I used it a few times, but not very often, and usually more or less we moved in the right direction.

Rasmussen is keen to point out I shouldn't interpret his having, and occasionally using, this nuclear weapon to mean that he didn't have a dialogue with ambassadors as well; he implies that it was just a rebalanced relationship. A rebalanced relationship involving more of the general and less of the secretary, perhaps? 'Yes! And that's because I think in general international organisations that are very much dependent on member states can only survive if they have a clear profile, and that includes a very clear profile of the leader.'

Over time, the profile of this leader was to become very clear on one issue in particular: Rasmussen's sharp and sustained criticism of Russia for its involvement in eastern Ukraine. Not everyone in NATO was happy with the manner in which he went about it, but Rasmussen insists that his policy towards Russia was understanding and nuanced.

When I first met President Putin in 2002, he was strongly pro-Western; he argued enthusiastically for a closer relationship between Russia and NATO and the West. But I think the Rose Revolution in Georgia in 2003 and the Orange Revolution in Ukraine in 2004 gave him the impression that the Americans in general and the CIA in particular intended to export those colour revolutions to Moscow, to get rid of him. He's a former KGB officer and very conspiratorial in his thinking, and he made the infamous statement in 2005 in a national state of the union speech that the biggest geopolitical catastrophe of the last century was the collapse of the Soviet Union.

Rasmussen gives a potted history of Russian initiatives around this time, culminating in the intervention in Georgia in 2008. 'Nevertheless, I stated that one of my priorities was that we should try and develop a strategic partnership between NATO and Russia. I was still convinced this could be a possibility, and actually in 2010 at a NATO–Russia summit we decided to develop such a strategic partnership.' Rasmussen pauses.

> But all that changed in 2014 when Putin attacked Ukraine and illegally included Crimea into the Russian Federation. We had to adapt to that, so I completely changed my attitude towards Russia. I'm not anti-Russian; actually, I do believe that the West and Russia have shared interests, economically and security-wise. But of course we cannot return to business as usual with Russia as long as the current leadership in the Kremlin destabilises the situation in Ukraine. So this is why I was very outspoken and I didn't have real problems within NATO in expressing those strong statements.

I ask Rasmussen whether he used his third 'weapon' as Secretary General – the personal relationships he'd cultivated with Prime Ministers, Presidents and Chancellors around NATO's members – a lot at this time. 'Yes, I spoke with many of them, I met with many of them, I travelled a lot. The general sense was that now NATO is back to basics. Now we have to strengthen our territorial defence in the East to protect ourselves against Russia.' Using his position at NATO to rally the troops, as it were. As he talks through the NATO rapid reaction plan and the rotating presence in eastern Allied countries, I'm struck by how far he's describing a role which by the end was almost entirely the general and almost none of the secretary.

Rasmussen left the job in 2014 and handed over the reins to another Ex Man, former Norwegian Prime Minister Jens Stoltenberg. His five years in command had offered a new model for how to be Secretary General, and while some grated at his outspokenness, it's hard to see NATO going back to the old way of doing things. But I have a final question. Bearing in mind he spent five years heading up a military alliance which confronted Russia over its military involvement in Ukraine, what does he make of efforts like those of Jean Chrétien and the InterAction Council to talk to Russia about a diplomatic solution? He starts by welcoming these kinds of initiatives, although he notes that 'I rarely see concrete outcomes of all those efforts'. And he tells me he's taken a markedly different approach. 'I believe that the only way to convince Russia, and for that matter other autocrats in the world, that they are better served by constructive co-operation rather than the destructive confrontation is to strengthen the voice of the world's free societies, the world's democracies,' he says.

To play his part, he's set up a non-profit which organises an annual democracy summit in Copenhagen, to gather political, business and civil society leaders to discuss and map out ways for democracies to work more closely together 'against the advancing autocracies that are threatening our liberal democracies'. The first year, he tells me, he brought Joe Biden, Tony Blair, former Prime Minister José María Aznar of Spain, former Prime Minister Stephen Harper of Canada, former President Felipe Calderón of Mexico and former President Toomas Ilves of Estonia. Behold, I think to myself, as he rattles through this list: the Ex Men's club in full working order; the direct result of that 'very broad international network' he so assiduously cultivated. In addition to these summits, Rasmussen's Alliance of Democracies Foundation organises training for young global leaders, monitors election integrity to help sniff out foreign interference, and works to ensure better economic opportunities. 'So it's a very broad effort to strengthen democracies both internally and to address the challenges coming from abroad.' At the risk of over-extending the military metaphor, in the battle for the heart and soul of global society, it sounds to me as though one-time General Rasmussen is now running his own paramilitary force, supporting democratic governments' regular troops? 'Yes, exactly. I've been in politics my whole life, more or less, and I strongly believe in deci-sive political leadership. But in addition to that I believe we need stronger private initiatives to fill the holes, so to speak.' It's also worth noting that this is the club, and these are the values, of the man who hopes to be the next President of the United States. And while a President Biden would certainly be spending most of his time with today's generation of leaders, if he is elected he will find a ready cadre of Ex Men with whom he still has much in common.

• • •

In terms of running international organisations, Rasmussen's gen-eration was prolific. During his time as Prime Minister of Denmark, former Italian Prime Minister Romano Prodi was President of the European Commission. Prodi was succeeded by former Portuguese Prime Minister José Manuel Barroso and eventually former Prime Minister of Luxembourg Jean-Claude Juncker. Meanwhile, Herman Van Rompuy was Prime Minister of Belgium and Donald Tusk was Prime Minister of Poland; the two men went on to be the first and second Presidents of the European Council respectively. It's a small world, and a reminder of the potential value of a broad network assiduously cultivated. This is particularly true in Europe, with a tradition of Ex Men taking up the very top jobs. In fact, the European Commission was run by a former Prime Minister for an unbroken spell of twenty-five years between 1995 and 2020. As President of the Council, Donald Tusk was succeeded by another Ex Man (and another former Belgian Prime Minister), Charles Michel. This is no coincidence, according to John Bruton, the former Irish Taoiseach, who has spent most of his political life deeply embedded in European politics. Bruton tells me that there's more to these Ex Men's appointments than personal relationships.

> We should not underestimate the importance of being part of a political family. Just as in a national political system there is party loyalty, and one tries to secure positions for people of one's own affiliation party-wise. The same thing applies at European level. And it is cultivated by personal relationships within the party. That's not to say that one can't have great relations with somebody from a different party, of course you can have good relationships with them. But in Europe the European People's Party (EPP) has been the biggest party for a while, and that was obviously an advantage to me, and would be an advantage to someone from whichever becomes the biggest party in the Parliament elections, which makes the Parliament elections quite important.

This partly explains why Tony Blair lost out to Herman Van Rompuy in their quest to be Presidents of the Council, according to academic Kevin Theakston. 'In the end, Blair lost out partly because the different EU heads of government decided to opt for a low-key "fixer" rather than a more weighty, charismatic and ambitious rival-figure,' Theakston wrote, 'and partly because, in the political deal that was struck, the post was claimed by Europe's centre-right parties.'³ No coincidence on this analysis, then, that the first woman to lead the European Commission, and the first in twenty-five years not to be an Ex Man, Ursula von der Leyen, is a member of the EPP.

The same pattern of Ex Men hanging around the top table can be seen on the other side of the Mediterranean, where the current chairperson of the African Union Commission is Moussa Faki Mahamat, a former Prime Minister of Chad. He was the second Ex Man to take on that job and, like Anders Fogh Rasmussen at NATO, part of his pitch was a promise to reform the AU bureaucracy. He's notable in having appointed a number of other Ex Men to jobs as 'high representatives' for various problems and trouble spots. On the other side of the Atlantic, several Ex Men have served as Secretary General of the Organization of American States, including César Gaviria, the former President of Colombia who co-chaired the Latin American Commission on Drugs and Democracy. Elsewhere in the world, Julia Gillard, the former Australian Prime Minister, has followed in the footsteps of Malcolm Fraser in running a major international NGO. She is chair of the Global Partnership for Education, a role which involves strategic oversight and, in particular, fundraising. Helle Thorning-Schmidt, a former Prime Minister of Denmark, spent a couple of years running Save the Children. And both Gillard and Thorning-Schmidt were members of Gordon Brown's Global Education commission.

When you reach the top, it is a very small world indeed, and what a difference it makes to have assiduously cultivated a broad network.

CHAPTER 6

THE DIPLOMAT

It's a very hot morning in June 2014 and I'm walking up quiet side streets past homes belonging to some of the world's wealthiest people. I'm in Mayfair, the smartest and most expensive district in central London, and I'm on my way to meet an Ex Man who has spent the past nine months travelling the world as a UN Special Envoy on climate change. Thankfully for me, he's stopping in London for a few days to attend a conference and has agreed to sit down for a chat while he's here. When I reach his apartment, John Kufuor fills the door. At seventy-six, he is still an imposing figure: tall, immaculately besuited and carrying a silver-tipped cane. He beckons me in, we settle into a pair of large armchairs and after cups of tea are brought through, his team retreat and busy themselves in the other room and we're left alone.

Ban Ki-moon, then UN Secretary General, has been quite prolific in anointing Ex Men as 'Special Envoys', but these roles seem a bit amorphous – a something and nothing job – and I'm hoping Kufuor might tell me a bit more about how they work. So I ask him if his job is simply about corralling his former colleagues in presidential palaces across the world into coming to the UN's climate change conference that autumn. 'The idea of the summit is to appeal to heads of state, CEOs of multinationals, to come,' he tells

me. Just to get them to the summit? 'Yes, yes, yes.' Not to take a view
at the summit, just to get them there? 'These people already have all
the experts to advise them on these matters, and I'm not a scientist.
And Ban Ki-moon has all these experts...' We're talking about leadership again, his primary concern when he left office and the focus
of most of his post-presidential attention. So how does he appeal
to these current leaders, arrest their attention? This wasn't left to
chance, Kufuor tells me. He was invited to take up this job at the
same time as Jens Stoltenberg, the former Norwegian Prime Minister.* And once they'd both accepted, they were taken to the least
retreat-sounding retreat I've ever heard of. 'All these department
heads and Ban Ki-moon and his deputy, the World Bank President,
they all came there and we got bombarded and within a day or two
my head was...' He mimes overload. 'We at least gleaned some of
the arguments to convince people of the urgency, to get prepared
a bit.' Kufuor is a well-regarded international figure, but especially
within Africa he knows all the leaders, so I ask whether the plan
was for him to focus on Africa while Stoltenberg took Europe, for
example, or whether they divided up the countries in some other
way. 'Initially the idea was for the two of us to move together', to
visit the European Union and then the African Union. 'When they
see Kufuor's face there, it is normal, but then they see Stoltenberg,
they see that this is global' – and vice versa. In reality, the shortage
of time has made this approach impossible, but I'm interested in
what happens once they get into these meetings. What does he say
to the current leaders when he meets them? 'Many of them know
the arguments', he replies. 'Sometimes the trouble is it's a matter of
prioritising for them.' For me, this is the nub of these appointments:

---

* Who in October 2014 became Secretary General of NATO; Mary Robinson was later
appointed the second Special Envoy on Climate Change.

presumably the reason the UN Secretary General appointed him and Stoltenberg rather than two climate change experts is that he can use his experience and understanding of how elective politics works to lay out the landscape and put his points in the relevant political context? 'You don't go presuming that the Presidents are not informed. That would be lecturing, and I don't think it would make the necessary impact. You just go to try to get them to give the urgency, pride of place, to climate change.' Because there's always an argument to be made for not giving it that urgency: 'Next year is my election so let me put this one aside, I do not know how my business community will accept this, that sort of thing. The idea of the summit is to bring everyone together and commit themselves to the world.' I ask him whether he appeals to their competitive instincts, and he tells me that they're all aware of the geopolitics around this, and the big emitters are all waiting to see what the others will do.

> At a World Bank meeting a month or two ago I had the opportunity to talk to a Chinese minister who had come, and to tell him that the invitation is for the President to come, and tell the world that China is doing quite a bit, developing renewables and so on, and is committed to cut back on emissions. They've decided on that themselves. But the appeal was that this should come from the mouth of the President, at this summit, to let the whole world know.

This is far from Kufuor's only job at this level, and he is an experienced international diplomat. In most of his jobs he will have a team of technical specialists, as well as lower-level diplomats, working with him. His job is to close the deal. I wonder whether part of his ability to do this is because, like Helen Clark, he's perceived to have done a good job of running his own country. He agrees. Does that help, I ask – the ability to say, 'Look, I've done this, I know how hard it is'? His answer is as clear as it is sharp. 'No, I wouldn't.' He doesn't use it, because it wouldn't help. 'Perhaps I've developed the intuition of how things work, [but] I can't pretend I know about their institution. So first accord them the wisdom and the commitment to do these things. In the current world people tend to have the statistics.' And then he gives me an example which intrigues me the more it goes on, because it is part of the Jimmy Carter guinea worm story, but a side I've not heard before.

Say your country is suffering the plight of guinea worms and river blindness. The world knows it, the WHO would have the detail: these bodies are set up to help fight these things. I remember when I was in power, Jimmy Carter came to visit many times. Ghana was endemic with guinea worms, and as you know guinea worm was a water-borne disease. So he came to Ghana quite a few times, thinking my government was not doing much. But my government had sourced a credit line of over $40 million to do the water works and the cure is potable water.

He slaps his leg.

So I remember once he came and he sounded rather too anxious, and I was trying to assure him, 'Mr President we're doing what we can,' and I got the feeling that perhaps he wasn't appreciating what I was trying to do. Eventually we finished the water works and now Ghana is free.

Kufuor tells me that he and Carter are now good friends, and he receives the credit for the work, but it taught him a lesson for his own post-presidency. 'From this I learned that you meet a President, of course he knows his problems, and the world knows the problems; if you want to appeal to him, don't assume he's not knowledgeable.' In other words, Kufuor is very clear about what he's there for. He needs to know the detail but he's not sent to deal with it. He is there to paint on a big canvas, to offer and encourage political leadership, but also to take seriously the credentials of the people he is dealing with. It's the same spirit, he tells me, that he brings to his other post-presidential activities, including as mediator and negotiator elsewhere in Africa. He has done that for the African Union, for the Commonwealth and for the UN; in Côte d'Ivoire, in Malawi and in Kenya. In all of them, he says, he was always careful to be above the political fray: 'The minute you allow yourself to become the pawn of anybody, you lose your moral position.'

•　•　•

'You need to be seen as being honest brokers, politically neutral, impartial, and these kinds of figures provide that.' For Patrick Merloe, director of election programs at the US National Democratic Institute (NDI), the importance of being an honest broker in his line of work is paramount. But it's not, on its own, sufficient. 'You need to be seen as independent of national interests of those you're representing, or geopolitical interests if you're inter-governmental, and these kinds of figures are also – because of their reputations – known to be independent actors. So it really helps reinforce the bona fides of the election observation.' Merloe is one of the most experienced figures in election monitoring. He was in Panama with Jimmy Carter and Gerald Ford more than thirty years ago and he's been organising missions ever since; fifteen years ago he helped write the international guidelines which largely determine how they are run.

Finding the right leader is one of the first tasks for anyone setting up an election observation delegation, which is why most organisations sending them look to one or more Ex Men. They'll bear in mind things like political balance, country knowledge, someone who will be accepted into the country and then, as Merloe says, 'access to the competitors – and well-known public figures from the political arena are important to be able to get that access'. Sir Don McKinnon is even more blunt. A gregarious former Deputy Prime Minister of New Zealand who was Secretary General of the Commonwealth for eight years, he regularly called upon Ex Men to lead election-monitoring missions. When I ask whether this access is an important part of their job, he replies simply, 'That is their task. They can get doors opened for them that no technocrat can ever do.' But how much of that ability to get access and to do all the things they need to do depends on the reputation of an individual Ex Man? How much is it the reputation of their country? Patrick Merloe answers by talking about Botswana, and two Ex Men in particular: Festus Mogae and Ketumile Masire. 'The respect for Botswana carries its own weight, and then the men themselves distinguished themselves as President and after their presidency based on their integrity, not just in elections but in other things,' he tells me. Masire was particularly important when the NDI went into Kenya after violence had scarred the country in 2007–08, because he had been involved in a peace initiative to end it. 'So we wanted him with us when we first went into the country,' recalls Merloe. 'All you had to say was "Quett Mesire" and people listened.'

But they also want to talk. 'I do have access,' Festus Mogae agrees when I ask him about this access to current political leaders during an election-monitoring mission. 'But people also want to see me, and people want to point out criticisms about one thing or another, and draw it to my attention. You need to watch out and to evaluate any complaints you receive.' Mogae tells me the key part of the job is to differentiate technical failure from attempted corruption, but he's modest about his reputation, while recognising that it's important for the work he does. 'It's delicate, but I have some experience now and some name and face recognition in Africa, so I humbly feel acceptable to colleagues and then the countries in which I become engaged with elections.'

'So sometimes it really is the personality, and it isn't that they're necessarily from a big country,' Pat Merloe continues. 'But then if you talk about [former South African President Thabo] Mbeki it's hard to separate out the importance that South Africa plays, particularly in southern Africa, in the relationships, from the personality.' Mbeki was not a particularly well-regarded President of his country but has won plaudits since leaving office for his diligent work around the continent. Festus Mogae worked closely with him in mediating a border dispute between Burundi and Tanzania, and agrees with that assessment.

He's a very able man. Therefore, when you work with him, he's logical, he argues his positions very logically, therefore it's a pleasure to work with him. When you are discussing and you are all being logical, then you have no hesitation admitting a point or raising a reservation on something else – it's open-minded and you're working as colleagues.

McKinnon agrees with much of Merloe's analysis but insists there can be other factors at play. 'When I went to visit President Mugabe and said that I hoped he would invite a Commonwealth observer mission to the elections coming up, we had a sixth sense there would be real problems,' McKinnon remembers.

> Sure enough, he said he would invite the Commonwealth to attend, and hoped we'd send very good people, and I said we certainly would send good people. So the one thing I wasn't going to do was to send a bunch of people from what is loosely described as the old Commonwealth. I didn't want to flaunt in his face people that he would just say 'these are a bunch of whites'. So I pretty much rounded up a team which was incredibly African-Caribbean-oriented, and it really didn't give him any opportunity to criticise the makeup of that team.

And then he says something telling. 'I don't think I ever got a request to send a senior Brit… They saw that as too much carrying a colonial banner.' Perhaps this explains, in part, why so few Western Ex Men are hired for these missions. Notable exceptions are Yves Leterme, the former Belgian Prime Minister who went on to run the NGO International Institute for Democracy and Electoral Assistance, and Lawrence Gonzi, the former Prime Minister of Malta who went to the Maldives on behalf of the Commonwealth in 2013. McKinnon saw Gonzi in operation there and was impressed. 'He soon won over Maldivians, even though he was anything but a Muslim,' McKinnon remembers. 'He was intelligent, he was smart, he came from a small island, which was very appropriate. He just got along with them very well, they knew that he was batting on their side.'

When I reach Gonzi via Zoom during the 2020 coronavirus lockdown, he laughs when I tell him what McKinnon said about his success in the Maldives. The two are old friends, and Gonzi suspects that McKinnon recommended him for that mission, so he doesn't demur when I explain McKinnon's analysis of the compatibility. The two island-states are both maritime nations, Gonzi tells me, both concerned about water and energy and the environment. Many of the challenges facing the Maldives in the early twenty-first century faced Malta twenty years earlier, he says, whether that is transitioning to modern democracy, modernising the economy or dealing with the influence of religion in politics. 'The Maldives is a strictly Islamic society. The Maldivian people are very, very religious, but Islamic,' he says. 'In Malta's case we are also religious, but Catholic, and the influence of religion on politics – I knew exactly what that meant because in past years Malta had gone through that situation. The Maldives were still going through that situation, which again made it easier for me to understand.' Gonzi believes that in 2013 this helped ease his relationship with Mohamed Nasheed, the former President who had just been forced out of office, and whom he'd first met when they were both still running their countries.

I could understand that language, I could understand those challenges, and he must have automatically assumed that I was understanding exactly what he was saying ... so immediately the chemistry worked. Whether it would have worked if it was someone else, if it was somebody from a larger country or with a different economic picture, I wouldn't be arrogant enough to make an assessment. But certainly, in my case, I can assess that the chemistry worked, which meant I could easily pick out what was wrong and where the dangers were.

This familiarity with some of the challenges facing developing nations, and ability to empathise rather than just sympathise, marks

Gonzi out. And perhaps it is another part of the explanation for the rather desultory turnout from Western European Ex Men on the election-monitoring circuit. If so, a third reason is that there is such a rich and varied platter of opportunities now on offer in the European Union. Aside from roles running the Commission and Council, from its earliest days Ex Men have taken on roles as Commissioners and in the Parliament. Former Belgian Prime Ministers have been particularly involved, about half having served in the European Parliament at some point. Paul-Henri Spaak was the first, a founding father of the forerunner to the EU, the European Coal and Steel Community; Leo Tindemans and Wilfried Martens both occupied senior roles in the European People's Party; Jean-Luc Dehaene became an important voice on the convention that prepared the EU Constitution; while Guy Verhofstadt was leader of the Alliance of Liberals and Democrats for Europe and served as the Parliament's Brexit coordinator. This pattern led two academics to conclude that for Belgian Prime Ministers, 'while it was certainly the peak of their political career, for most it was an unexpected intermezzo, but not the end'.[1] However, arguably the most significant contribution made by an Ex Man in Europe, short of being President of the Commission or European Council, was by a French Ex Man. Valéry Giscard d'Estaing, after serving a single term as President of France in the 1970s, retreated into French local government for almost two decades. Then, in 2001, twenty years after losing office, he was plucked again from obscurity and asked to preside over the Convention on the Future of Europe, which drafted the new European Constitution.

On the other side of the Mediterranean, there's been a concerted campaign to encourage opportunities for successful leaders when they become Ex Men. In part because it's a waste not to utilise the experience and skills of knowledgeable men and women within Africa; in part because, as telecoms tycoon Mo Ibrahim emphasised when he endowed his eponymous $5 million prize for Achievement in African Leadership, it might incentivise good governance while still in office. Mary Robinson has been on the prize committee since it was inaugurated, and she explains some of Ibrahim's thinking to me. 'There was a lot of debate at the beginning, when I joined, first of all about a prize, and why so big a prize,' she recalls.

> Mo was adamant on that. He said, 'Good leadership in Africa is priceless. African leaders who abuse their office can get far more than the Mo Ibrahim prize, but African leaders have responsibilities that go well beyond. First of all, the responsibility as leaders, it's much more difficult day by day … but even afterwards African leaders have dependants beyond immediate family, and if we want them to be encouraged to serve well and then step down, this will encourage them to serve well and then step down.'

The prize has been awarded only six times in twelve years, and Festus Mogae, one of those six, now chairs the award committee. 'Of course it is a matter of regret when it appears we are not making enough of the progress we thought we were making,' he tells me when I ask in 2020 why so few African Ex Men have been deemed worthy winners, 'but nevertheless it is based on principles.' When he won, in 2008, the prize was just a year old, and he confesses to having been surprised. 'It came as a surprise and a pleasant one. I'd never heard of the man, Mo Ibrahim.' This in turn startles me – if he and his fellow Ex Men, and more importantly the current leaders, don't know about it, how can it help persuade them to lead well? He tells me that times have changed: today 'they had heard of it.

Colleagues know about it, most former Presidents like me but also Presidents who are in office, and it is talked about.' Mogae tells me this is particularly true in southern and in Anglophone Africa. 'I think it has some influence. I can't say exactly how much, but it certainly has. I would say it would be surprising if current leaders don't think about it and wonder what is the best thing to do.' Thinking about it and wondering is very different from changing your behaviour, though, and Joe Clark, the former Canadian Prime Minister, who travels widely in Africa, told me when we spoke the year before that its influence on incumbent leaders seems to be declining. If so, all is not lost, because Robinson and Mogae agree on the growing importance of another part of the Ibrahim project: the Index of African Governance, a tool which measures and monitors governance performance. Mogae believes it is appreciated by citizens: 'I think expectations about leadership [are set] on that basis.' But there is another lens through which one can look at African Ex Men: one which sees them as a highly valuable resource.

●　●　●

It's early November 2010 and Charles Stith, a former US Ambassador to Tanzania, is handing me a bright red Boston University folder bulging with documents about his African Presidential Center. In one there's a photocopied letter from Kofi Annan, on UN Secretary General's notepaper, calling Stith's initiative 'a unique and important contribution to encouraging democratization on the continent', so I'm intrigued to hear more about this unique contribution. Stith is a salesman, an enthusiast, and he believes he's identified not only a way to incentivise good governance but also a route to putting these Ex Men to better use. 'There is no way to institutionalise the office, to validate the office, without validating and affirming the people who served in that office,' he tells me when once we've sat down. It's a bald statement and once he makes it, everything else he's working on makes sense. The programmes he runs, from an annual President-in-Residence programme to former Presidents' round-tables, are all based on this simple idea. Over the past few years he's hosted Festus Mogae, Jakaya Kikwete of Tanzania and Kenneth Kaunda of Zambia at the university, as well as holding roundtables in different cities around the world. And Kofi Annan isn't the only person to see the merits of these initiatives. When I ask Olusegun Obasanjo about Stith's approach, he nods in recognition. 'The office is important, the office must be hallowed. Now by hallowing the office you are hallowing those who have occupied the office.' And then he tells me about a visit he made to Frederick Chiluba, the second President of Zambia. 'He was making life unbearable for Kaunda [his predecessor]. And I went to him and said, "Look, you will be the first President who had to deal with a past President, and whatever measure you dealt out to the past President will be used in dealing out to you."' Obasanjo pauses, no doubt bringing to mind a later visit to Zambia, this time trying to find an accommodation between Chiluba and his successor, before finishing his thoughts. 'And it was almost prophetic.' Obasanjo is keen to emphasise that Ex Men should not be hallowed regardless of conduct, and Mo Ibrahim's and Charles Stith's outfits likewise honour only demo-crats – that's the point of them. But there are of course grey areas. Should Ex Men expect to receive stipends and pensions from the state? How generous should they be? And what should happen if an Ex Man is found guilty of theft? These are all live questions, not just in Africa but across the world, although they're more immediate in Africa because the democracies are younger, the institutions and

their holders less hallowed. At least one African Ex Man has com-
plained to me about his benefits being withheld by the political
opponents who succeeded him, and these stories appear regularly
in newspapers across the continent. But Ex Men offer much more
than just examples to be hallowed, according to Obasanjo. 'Africa
is politically, and particularly in terms of development, whether we
are talking of democratic development and process, or physical development, or social development, Africa is still very much a young
continent,' he says. 'So the idea of a leader leaving power and not
still being able to contribute, it might be a waste.'

'These are tremendous assets,' Charles Stith agrees. 'These guys
tend to be bright, they understand power, they clearly understand
politics, and the other thing is they have a perspective, a vantage
point if you will, that very few other people share, which is why
former Presidents tend to get along with former Presidents very
well.' And so, as he set up his Center, Stith started asking how these
Ex Men could be put to better use. As we talk, he offers me numerous examples of Ex Men doing useful work in Africa. And since
then, leaders like John Kufuor have been hired by the UN, while
the list of African Union High Representatives for particularly challenging issues currently includes five Ex Men, from Burundi, Mali,
South Africa, Togo and Kenya. Obasanjo has become a roving mediator, including as a UN Special Envoy on the Great Lakes region,
and has chaired the West Africa Drug Commission, the regional
franchise of the Global and Latin American commissions. But these
Ex Men aren't used just because they're available, or because they're
high-profile, but because their experience at the top table makes
them better able to connect with current leaders – even bearing in
mind John Kufuor's caution about being respectful. 'You can often
be very effective in making a point because you know how to frame

what to say in terms that will be most congenial to the person you're speaking to, how to put their head on your shoulders, to understand what are the forces influencing that person,' former Canadian Prime Minister Kim Campbell tells me.

It's just common sense, but I think democratic politicians under-stand instinctively what the pressures are on somebody at the top, and therefore you can often be an effective advocate because you can speak in terms that will resonate with another political leader. But that doesn't guarantee that you will be effective.

That can be particularly important where the job at hand is mediation.

•   •   •

'You kind of feel honour-bound to do your best when you are asked to do something which, if it were to work, enhances peace between your fellow African countries.' Festus Mogae's involvement in me-diating the border dispute between Burundi and Tanzania sounds both draining and dispiriting. 'But you cannot know for certain what people are going to feel, therefore you take it on the basis that it is an attempt to do the right thing, it may or may not work.' And in this case it hasn't, despite the involvement of not just Mogae and Mbeki but former Tanzanian President Joaquim Chissano as well. But Mogae tells me that's what you sign up for.

You try to see two divergent positions, you try to reconcile them. But it's not easy. With boundary disputes they tend to be intran-sigent. I suppose it's politically difficult to admit to your own electorate. Unfortunately, what people do is they politicise it from the very beginning, and that takes away their own flexibility for them to be open-minded.

As he describes his approach, it sounds a lot to me like therapy, which I suppose it is. 'You have to be as fair as possible, and courteous,' he says.

> You'd say, 'Supposing this is the case and that is the case, would it not be better to go this way?' because again there is always the danger of being accused of favouring the other side, which you shouldn't do, but you can't but point out certain plausible positions that one side might be taking, and the implausibility that the others are taking. But of course you can't say, 'No, no, yours is impossible.' You ask questions. And a lot of patience, a lot of patience! Some delegations would have members among them who are totally irrational, and talk nonsense, but you can't say, 'You're talking nonsense!'

As he talks about patience, I'm reminded of the session about Russia and Ukraine at the InterAction Council meeting. Mogae laughs as I ask him whether, after a hard day, he, Mbeki and Chissano would get together after hours to blow off steam, and he agrees. But he also describes an after-hours session which is heads-down, with a focus on possible political breakthroughs. And I suppose whether it's Lawrence Gonzi, chosen for his match to politicians in the Maldives, or Mogae, Chissano and Mbeki, chosen to bring their weight to bear in the dispute between Burundi and Tanzania, these Ex Men always wear their political hats. Their understanding always springs from their political background; their status means the participants find it much harder to walk away from the table. It's the basis for much of The Elders' work, and for Jimmy Carter's success everywhere in the world he's ever been – including incredibly tense and dangerous missions to Haiti and North Korea.

•   •   •

'It's an entirely different level of pressure and stress compared to being Prime Minister, but you're still engaged at a high level in issues that are important to New Zealand.' Back at the hotel in Wales, the former New Zealand Prime Minister Jim Bolger is talking to me about his time as his country's top diplomatic representative to the United States. 'The plus for a small country of having a former Prime Minister there – there's approaching 200 ambassadors – this clearly gives you an edge in terms of being familiar with a number of the key figures in the administration, which I was: I knew them well.' If you want to get attention for whatever issue is important to your country when there are 190 others who also want to claim attention from senior officials, that could be crucial, but could he have done the same if he hadn't been Prime Minister? Or did his skillset, and his background, combine to deliver things for New Zealand which nobody else could have? 'I absolutely believe that, but you can never absolutely prove it.' Bolger tells me about a meeting he'd had with Bill Clinton during his premiership, where he had picked his moment at a regional summit, strode up and done a good deal of government business, and got some significant changes of policy from the United States. 'So you changed it all in – I don't know – a ten-minute conversation at the stern of a boat as you're sailing across the harbour,' he says. 'And that's part of the skill, to have people who can quietly but confidently engage with people that you want to engage with.' And although in that meeting there were specific policy goals he wanted to accomplish, his broader agenda was an improvement in the New Zealand–US relationship, which had been very poor during the 1980s because of his country's anti-nuclear stance. Improving that relationship was the focus of his time as Ambassador, too. 'I was able to establish personal relations to the senior players who would ultimately be advising the political leadership,' he goes on, 'and then I continued in chairing the New Zealand–US council and before I left Washington I set up the US–New Zealand council. And it's now considered a major forum for the two countries to participate in.'

New Zealand has a long history of despatching its former Prime Ministers to its most powerful overseas diplomatic postings, and just a few years after Bolger's return, New Zealand appointed Mike Moore, whom Bolger had defeated in the 1990 general election, to its embassy in Washington DC. When I reach him by phone, I ask Moore what he makes of Bolger's analysis. 'I think he's probably right on that,' he says, before adding quickly, 'but don't overestimate the power New Zealand has. In Washington you're one of hundreds, and there's a pecking order in it. It's what use you can be made of, not what use you can make of them.' He begins to break down the structure of political society in Washington, from the think tanks to the social networks. 'Who knows him, who's his best friend,' and then, perhaps the most important question, 'where does he get his money from?' But the reason to send a former politician, particularly an Ex Man, is the perception that they can short-circuit some of the political order, isn't it?

Yes, that's right. But it's also ensuring that if you have people for dinner it's a good dinner, it's not a bullshit dinner! They've got to enjoy themselves, they've got to be rollicking with laughter at the end of it. So I got quite a few senior ministers, senior officials, to my place, and I got quite a good reputation for having a bloody good party.

Access to the corridors of power and familiarity with the key players in an administration, bloody good party or not, is only part of an Ambassador's job, though. There's a second major source of power in the city, often overlooked, and for John Bruton, who for five years was the European Union Ambassador to Washington, that was his target. 'I found being Ambassador in the United States to be tremendously interesting for a former politician, and particularly a former Prime Minister,' Bruton tells me.

Because unlike other ambassadorial roles, you're not just dealing with civil servants, with senior diplomats, but you're dealing with Congress. So I decided to devote my attention particularly to Congress, and to get to know and to meet with, if possible, every member of Congress, which is a lot of people. Now, I didn't meet them all, but I met a very large number of them.

And that's not easy. 'To contrive to get to meet a congressman from Texas or a congressman from Idaho, you had to work very hard at finding some connection between their state and the European Union,' he laughs, 'but I managed it.' He wanted to explain the EU to Americans, which he found easier than explaining it to Europeans. 'You can compare the Commission with the administration, the House of Representatives with the European Parliament...' and so on. 'Americans have a sort of mental architecture in their mind which you can use to represent the European Union, which is more difficult to do in Britain or Ireland.'

Bruton had always taken an interest in the EU and had an emotional connection which went beyond national self-interest, taking care to nurture his party's relationship with its wider European political family, the European People's Party. Then, after losing office in 1997, he joined the Dáil's European Committee, which published a report on potential future treaty change in the EU. 'That report made me a candidate to represent the Dáil in the Convention on the Future of Europe,' Bruton tells me.

> Then the opportunity of somebody being representative of the national Parliaments on the presidium of the convention came up, and as a former Prime Minister and one of the EPP representatives, I was a pretty credible candidate for that job, and I got it. So I was one of two representatives, the other of whom was Gisela Stuart, who subsequently lost the faith, shall we say.

He laughs again. That's putting it mildly: Stuart, a Labour MP for Birmingham, ended up as her party's most vocal critic of the European Union during the Brexit referendum. For Bruton, though, it was the start of a deepening relationship. 'That was really a tremendous experience. It was only a year, but because we were dealing with the entire set of treaties that governed the European Union, I acquired some familiarity with all the moving parts of the European Union.' And of course he was an Ex Man, with all the skills that had got him to the very top of Irish politics. 'I got some attention at European level because I was in the Convention and used the skills I had acquired at home to promote a particular view of the European Union, which commended itself to others.' Evidently it commended itself to some of the EU's most senior officials, because eventually an invitation to take the ambassadorial job materialised, where he would get the chance to promote that view of the European Union even more widely.

Ambassadors to Washington always have the opportunity to spend time explaining their country or institution to Congress, but what interests me, I tell Bruton, is that he invested so much time in meeting them, and that they wanted to meet him. How much of a difference does he thinks it made being a former Taoiseach?

The fact that I was a former Taoiseach made a big difference. The fact that I had addressed a joint session of Congress would have made a difference. The fact that I was Irish made a huge difference, because everybody in the United States has an Irish great-grand-mother or knows someone who has an Irish great-grandmother. The Irish projection is very high.

But there was more to it than that.

I'm interested in elections, I'm interested in politicians, I'm inter-ested in political geography, so I could talk about congressional races in South Carolina in the same way as I could talk about a selection convention in Sligo–Leitrim. If you get that interest in retail politics in one country, it's easy to carry it over into another. I never found that boring.

I tell Bruton I've always assumed there's something about elective politics which instils an ability to connect with other politicians who have to face their voters, and he nods.

The other thing I felt – I sympathised with them, and they sympa-thised with me. I knew that they were people that lived with the possibility of losing their seat every time they stood for election. And that's a special kind of risk-accepting lifestyle which I had had and they have. So you have something in common.

I think this is an underrated insight, and it describes an important part of what an Ex Man can bring not just to diplomacy but to any of the other roles described in this book.

• • •

Post-presidential organisations and meetings have the tendency to mirror what happens in the actual presidential meetings. That means the weight of the country you belong to is very important. Sometimes you can get normal people from big countries, and that makes them big leaders. Sometimes you have very good leaders in small countries, and that makes them special, not necessarily big players, but special.

Jamil Mahuad is a former President of Ecuador, and over breakfast in a noisy restaurant just outside Boston, where he has lived in exile since being overthrown in a coup, he is describing the power dynamic amongst Ex Men. I think there's a lot in what he says, but it's also noticeable how much diplomacy is conducted, and many international organisations run, by Ex Men from small (or smallish) countries. So for every Jimmy Carter, Nelson Mandela or Olusegun Obasanjo there are several Mary Robinsons, John Brutons and Festus Mogaes. There's Carl Bildt, the former Swedish Prime Minister who helped end the war in Bosnia, and Martti Ahtisaari, the former Finnish President who won the Nobel Peace Prize for his work in ending wars in Kosovo, Namibia and Aceh. It's actually rather difficult to think of any international organisation which is or has been run by the former leader of a major country. And Helen Clark thinks she has at least a partial explanation. After noting that she was appointed by Ban Ki-moon alongside Michelle Bachelet, the former President of Chile, she says she thinks it would have been harder for him to appoint Ex Men from large countries. 'Bigger countries tend to go with bigger egos, but for people from smaller countries, whether the New Zealands, the Portugals, the Chiles, the Irelands, and also I think particularly with those with an experience of Cabinet government, you can slot into a multilateral role more easily.' But this over-representation of Ex Men from smaller countries in international roles also comes back to what Pat Merloe said about the need to be 'honest brokers, politically neutral, impartial'. If someone from a smaller country is, as Jamil Mahuad puts it, 'a very good leader ... special', then they seem to hit a sweet spot which makes them eligible for really interesting international work. As Mahuad puts it:

I always try to recognise the two sides: one, the weight of the country, realpolitik, and the other, the quality of the man. One of the gifts we have as former Presidents is the time to reflect and the time to connect in more human terms with colleagues. And that is where the personal qualities are more evident for everybody.

CHAPTER 7

CONSCIENCE

Travelling north by train along the western shore of Lake Geneva, it doesn't take long to leave the city behind. If you're lucky enough to do this on a bright summer morning, you'll be rewarded with a spectacular view of the lake glittering on one side and of the steep, verdant hillside of the Swiss Alps, dotted with the homes of the rich, the very rich, and the incredibly rich on the other. It is truly beautiful and, since you're travelling against the rush in a mostly empty carriage, rather peaceful, too. Taking this journey on a sunny July morning in 2009, I ponder how appropriate it is that I should be just outside Geneva, with its cluster of international organisations and history as the home of the Universal Declaration of Human Rights and the League of Nations, the forerunner to today's UN. Because the man I'm travelling to meet has a history irrevocably bound up with questions of sovereignty, human rights and the obligations of the international community.

But I also need to pay attention to why I'm here; not easy with this history and this scenery. One question is bothering me, and it's one with which I've been wrestling for weeks. I'd ducked it during my interview request, and it has rarely been far from my mind as I did my research, booked my flights, and even as I wandered Geneva the night before in a fruitless search for a good ice cream.

The question is how I should address the man I'm on my way to meet: what should I call him? Now, this may seem like a marginal point, pedantic perhaps and possibly even prissy. Bearing in mind I'm hoping he will discuss his relationship with his cousin Queen Elizabeth II, tell me the story of how he expelled the Nazis from his country, and describe what living in exile for sixty years has done to his soul, the form of address could at first glance appear beside the point. But for Michael I, the former King of Romania, it very much is the point. Forced to abdicate in 1947, sixty-two years later he still believes himself to be King of the Romanians, and he shapes his role in public life accordingly. So the question of whether to greet him with a bow and address him as 'Your Majesty' hints at a much deeper question, central to him and to some of the themes of this book.

This deeper question, of the ongoing role Ex Men play in their national public life, presents an important dynamic. They can expect – like former British Prime Ministers Tony Blair and John Major on Brexit, or former Australian Prime Ministers Malcolm Fraser and Tony Abbott on indigenous rights – for their words to be heard. They sometimes – like former French Presidents and former Belgian and Israeli Prime Ministers – continue to play a domestic role, either politically or constitutionally. But in countries without a robust democratic tradition, their role in national public life can be even more important. In countries from Poland to the Maldives, Peru to Malaysia, what they stand for – or stand up for – often really matters.

This is what's really on my mind as the Swiss Railways train makes its way down the track towards Aubonne on this bright summer morning. Eventually, we pull into the station, and as I step into the fresh morning air, I am met by Constanta Iorga. Cheery, friendly and delighted to be working for the King, she's been in touch with me for several weeks, discussing the questions I'll soon be asking. She has kindly offered to ferry me from the station up to the King's house, and as we wend our way up into the hills, the mountains frame the other side of the lake, Mont Blanc winking in the distance as we round each bend. After a few minutes, we pass a small farmhouse and pull up outside a large, modern chalet-style home and I get out. Constanta tells me to head over to the door and, my ethical dilemma still dancing around my consciousness, I ring the doorbell and look around, waiting for someone to open it and bring me to King Michael. I don't have long to wait, and as the door opens and I step from the bright light into the dark hallway, I'm greeted by a very tall man who shakes hands and invites me to follow him through into the house. I almost ask if the King is through here, but I'm glad I don't because it soon becomes clear that this is the King. And by then, the moment for resolution of my ethical dilemma has more than passed.

Michael I was King of Romania for two short spells, between 1927 and 1930, and again between 1940 and 1947. For the first he was a boy king, only five years old at the start and not governing himself. But by the second, which began and ended during a time of unprecedented international turmoil, he was to lead his country in its complicated relationship with two of the twentieth century's most infamous totalitarian dictatorships. His reputation has been defined by his response to them. The Nazis were first. For four years this quiet, studious young man felt helpless to act against the Prime Minister, Ion Antonescu, who had taken his country into war alongside the Nazis. And then in 1944, sensing both possibility and the imminent collapse of the Nazi war machine throughout Eastern Europe, Michael dismissed Antonescu and switched Romania to the Allied side. It is often referred to as a coup d'état, but Michael bristles when I use this phrase. 'What happened on 23 August 1944 is not a coup,' he insists. 'As head of the country, I don't make coups. I had the right under our constitution to change the Prime Minister.' Most changes of government don't have quite such life-or-death consequences for the head of state or historical consequences for their country, and nor are they conducted in such an oppressive atmosphere or with such an air of conspiracy, but after fifty years of attacks from Romania's communists, Michael takes issue with any terminology that questions the legitimacy or constitutionality of his endeavours.

The day I travel to see him in his house just outside Geneva, all of this darkness feels a very long way away. It is beautifully bright and sunny, a delightful change from the typically foul summer weather that has been plaguing London. And the sitting room into which Michael has brought us has a wonderful view out over the valley below. Tea and coffee are waiting on a dainty tea set, but they remain untouched as the King and I – a phrase I will never get accustomed to and which even as I write this brings to mind visions of Deborah Kerr and Yul Brynner – sit down and immediately start talking. Michael's story is not only remarkable; it is unique amongst the former leaders in this book. He was the youngest person to have taken office, and the youngest to lose it. He was the only constitutional monarch to lead his people personally during the Second World War. And despite being relieved of office so young, he has lived a very full life, and is unusual in having had several 'real' jobs – including aeroplane test pilot, stockbroker and market gardener – while managing to retain the dignity of the former office he was raised to hold. Ivor Porter, a former British diplomat who met Michael during the war and later wrote a biography of him, presents an unfailingly flattering portrait of Romania's former monarch, and I rapidly understand why.[1] Michael is quiet, dignified and modest. From the story of his leadership against the Nazis and Stalinists alike, one can sense that he possesses considerable moral and physical courage.

But I'm here because of what Michael did after leaving office, and in how far he continued to affect Romania's destiny after his exile overseas. I think what he did during those long years of exile is a model increasingly being followed by Ex Men today, and it's playing an important part both within their countries and outside. But to understand why, I first need to get to the bottom of why he was relieved of his duties. And he wants to emphasise just how involuntary that was. 'The whole thing was done through blackmail,' he says of his enforced abdication at the very end of 1947. The situation in Romania had been getting progressively worse during the course of the previous three years, as the Red Army occupied the country and various of Stalin's henchmen, familiar to any student of the terror in the early Soviet Union, made their presence felt in Romania. The key moment was the arrival in February 1945 of Andrei Vyshinsky, who forced King Michael to appoint a communist-dominated government. This was led by Prime Minister Petru Groza, and it was he, with the communist leader Gheorghe Gheorghiu-Dej, who appeared in King Michael's study on 30 December two years later. 'They said if I didn't hurry up and sign this thing they were going to shoot over 1,000 young students that were kept in prison that had a big [demonstration] for me,' he recalls.

> I told them very clearly, that was a responsibility I could not take on myself for that sort of thing. And besides all these little details, if you like to look it up, you can see [that] the text was entirely

illegal, not just from a moral point of view but from a constitutional point of view ... And then they surrounded the house
with artillery, with Romanian former prisoners of war, they came
and took my guards away and they were all dressed in Russian
uniforms, the telephones were cut. What do you want to do then?

He signed, and in the early hours of 1948 the now officially ex-King
was ushered onto a train at his chilly Sinaia estate high up in the Car-
pathian mountains, guards standing at the end of each carriage and
blinds pulled down lest his people see him passing in the night. The
communists had hoped that none of this would be necessary, that
King Michael would simply fail to return from his first overseas trip
– to London in late 1947 for Princess Elizabeth's wedding. But just
as Hitler had underestimated Michael, so Stalin and his Romanian
vassals had now made the same mistake. Still, the history books are
not replete with examples of Kremlin embarrassment over displays
of naked power, and there would be none this time. Michael was
exiled, and his final train journey would serve as a grim metaphor
for what was to come in the weeks, months and years that followed,
as the communists went about painting him out of the picture. The
Romanian people suffered for forty-two years with post-war Europe's most brutal government. Michael would spend the rest of his
life trying to find his place in the world.

To start with, there was the psychological dislocation the King
felt from his people. Michael's wife, Queen Anne, wrote later that 'it
took the King about ten years to find himself again'; that their first
three daughters 'had to grow up with a kind, just, loving father who
was also a very silent, serious and sad one'.[2] Michael himself tells
me he wasn't depressed about the situation: 'If you get depressed
in that sense then it acts on you, it loses your initiative afterwards.

We didn't get depressed, we got very worried, disliking this intensely what they had done, but we had to sort of wait and see, that's about all we could do at the time.' But I'm not sure it's something he ever really got over. When he was able finally to return to Romania in 1992, he stood before an enormous crowd in Bucharest and told them simply, 'I love you all. Don't forget that.' And King or not, during Romania's dark years its people needed someone who loved them. Their experience under communism was amongst the worst of any in Eastern Europe. Because the Communist Party had shallower roots than anywhere else in Europe, to assert itself it resorted to the complete dismemberment of society and its reconstitution in its own mould. After the 1950s, when the Russians withdrew, the Romanian Communist Party was largely self-sufficient. The crimes perpetrated from then on were by Romanians on Romanians, and the deliberate crushing of the human spirit would become a uniquely awful characteristic of the regime. But alongside the hardline Marxism sat extreme nationalism and a bizarre form of autarky which led to ghastly social experiments with population growth. Abortion was banned and women were regularly inspected by government agents nicknamed the 'menstrual police' to see whether they were getting pregnant. But after conception the state offered only inadequate healthcare and doctrinal nonsense. Underweight babies were deemed miscarriages and unwanted survivors often ended up in orphanages. When the regime finally fell, and the Iron Curtain was pulled back, the sharp light of public scrutiny flooded in to reveal a system where society's unwanted – orphans and the elderly – were kept in bestial conditions. The outside world was finally shocked into action, and even now King Michael is clearly angry and distressed when he talks about it. What was so frustrating for him at the time, and reveals his utter powerlessness and lack of influence, was that no one he spoke to was prepared to do anything about it when it was still happening. The communists, he says, had 'this incredible strength to infiltrate and frighten … politics abroad, outside. They were very clever.' And in his mind, he is still asking why.

> Some people from here, I think, and other places, did come to have a look, but that was about all. Why couldn't they have done something more drastic or strong, banged their fists on the table for certain things? But they didn't. I'm not trying to be ungrateful for some things, but a little something more encouraging we would have hoped for.

These reflections on power and moral authority, issued in Michael's slightly muffled voice, echo those from Vaira Vīķe-Freiberga and Viktor Yushchenko about modern Russia, of course.

And this miserable response to terrible stories emanating from Romania was very similar to the reaction King Michael got more generally. At first it wasn't so bad – the family, in particular, rallied around. 'All our families, cousins and all that, there was never, ever any problem to see us, meet us, be with us, never,' he says. His wife, Queen Anne, is part of the Danish royal family and they are related to almost every royal family in Europe. George VI of Britain was the first to send an Ambassador to meet Michael in Switzerland, and over the next few years Michael would see him and his family regularly. When Queen Elizabeth succeeded to the throne, Michael, Queen Anne and their children would continue to be welcome at Balmoral Castle and the other royal estates. Did family relations go beyond meetings to firm political action, working with them in common cause? 'I wouldn't say we worked with them, because each country has their own way of doing things,' says Michael. 'But we used to meet occasionally – not often, but quite a few times.' The political activities were soon under way – speaking on the BBC and the Voice of America network, and working with the pre-war democrats, also now in exile. Through all this, Michael's main aim was simple: 'To keep the spirit going in Romania.' But this approach seemed premised on a speedy collapse of communism in Romania, and when that didn't happen the spirit began to wane. Eventually the people and the money also fell away, and Michael says his experience during this period was 'very unpleasant, very saddening'. 'When things happen like what happened with us, that's when you get to know your real friends, you know,' he snorts. 'Suddenly nobody knows you any more.' Over time, even the invitations to speak to serving leaders would dry up: 'I met a lot that were going to be or had been, but never when they were in [office], because it might have been taken badly by those others,' as he always refers to the communists. Michael continued to speak publicly when he could, but the opportunities to do that were increasingly limited too. He even had a case of someone who told him bluntly, 'You've got to understand, from now on, you're nothing.' 'Very pleasant to say that, no?' he asks, wearily.

If the political and psychological challenges King Michael faced were daunting, the financial one was almost as great. He had been prevented from bringing any money out of Romania, so he had to work. He rejected a generous financial offer to settle in the United States because he believed it would make him beholden to the CIA. But what could he do? Over the next couple of decades, and always alongside his role for the Romanian diaspora, Michael did a number of different jobs. But he never stopped considering himself King. Presumably he had to be careful with what he did? 'We were very careful not to do some things that might look a bit awkward. But the fact that we had a kitchen garden or had hens, or that sort of thing, there was nothing wrong with that.' So he avoided anything that reeked of selling out, and instead settled for something else: for a time he was a market gardener in the small town of Ayot St Lawrence in southern England (a wealthy Romanian exile was paying the school fees for his five children, so the financial challenge wasn't as daunting as for other Romanian exiles). He worked as a test pilot for Lear Jets and eventually wound up as a stockbroker at the New York firm of Droulia and Company, where he was known as Mr Michael King. And he spoke up: when I finish the interview, Constanta hands me a blue folder stamped with the royal crest containing several of his speeches from the early 1990s. In them, he lays bare for Western audiences what has happened to his fellow countrymen. Romania, he says, has 'passed through an unprecedented process of national degradation'; the death rate has increased every year under communist rule; 'my countrymen have lost hope and this is what makes the situation there tragic and unbearable'. The transition to what he calls 'the post-totalitarian society' must, he says, be 'an act of moral regeneration', which entails 'the rebirth of civil society, with its moral values; it entails a moral reconstruction of society, the restoration of civic awareness, the renewal of democratic debate and the crystallisation of political plurality in the broadest sense'. The language of liberal democracy, of globalisation, feels real and essential on these pages.

Michael's painful exile didn't end with the fall of Romanian communism and the bloody executions of Nicolae and Elena Ceaușescu on Christmas Day 1989. It was three years before he was even allowed back into the country, when he received a rapturous reception from hundreds of thousands of Romanians, for whom he remained a lonely symbol of Romania's shattered moral authority.

But that great outpouring of grief and love put the frighteners on the new regime in Romania, not so very different from the old one, and Michael was barred from visiting again until a new President was elected in 1997. By then his role had become clearer, but from as early as September 1990 his speeches contain a real urgency to his pleas that the West not forget Eastern Europe. Yes, he says repeatedly, by all means confront the tyranny in the Middle East (Saddam Hussein had just invaded Kuwait). Yes, by all means address the lingering danger of the Soviet Union. Yes, of course you must prepare yourselves for the recession. But don't ignore us. We are European, too, just without the benefit of the past forty-five years. 'Eastern Europe is today precisely where you left it in 1945. It faces problems of economic and political reconstruction and the task of clearing the rubble after a lengthy disaster,' he said in a speech in London in September 1990. That means we share all of the same values as you do in the West:

> Throughout the last forty-three years spent in forced exile, I have learnt to endure calumny, humiliation and threats to the life of my family. Yet nothing pained me more than hearing an idea – to which many in the West subscribed – according to which Romanians do not understand the meaning of democracy; they would be content with any system of government, as long as it supplied them with basic food and heating … My countrymen are neither backward nor naturally inclined towards dictatorships. Their present economic predicament may be unique on the European continent, but that is hardly their personal fault.

It was and remains a sharp rejoinder to debates about the suitability of Eastern European countries for joining the European bodies.

And that wasn't all: warm words are nice, but they won't be enough, said the Romanian King. Like Western Europe in 1945, Romania and her neighbours need a wealthy benefactor to deliver something akin to a Marshall Plan for Eastern Europe.

In these speeches Michael set out to do what the political leadership of his country at the time could or would not do: assert Romania's material and spiritual needs, her strategic importance and the moral debt owed by the West for the betrayals at the end of the Second World War, when Romania was bargained away to Stalin. Above all, though, he sought to remind each of his audiences that Romania is a part of Europe. 'The fathers of your economic community called their structure "European", he reminded those in London.

> Yet when I frequently point out to people that Europe does not end at the Alps, I usually get the reply that it is difficult to define the borders of the continent. Indeed it is, for much depends on our readiness to accept and accommodate change, to discard our former preconceived notions and to amend our calculations.

The past fifty years have been a ghastly aberration, he is saying, and we need you to help us overcome its legacy so we can rejoin you. He is doing something else, though. He clearly believes that the key to Romania's domestic salvation lies in its international position; that once inside NATO and the EU, the bright light of liberal democratic day would sweep away the last vestiges of Romania's dark communist night.

In this time of flux, Michael found renewed purpose as a leader. And the role as international advocate seems to have suited him well, for he continued in it for the next fifteen years. In the early stages it was clearly in spite of successive Romanian governments, but later, after he had been at least in part reconciled with his country's political class, it was in concert with them. But always the goal would be the same: helping recover Romania's position in Europe's family of nations and using that position to force domestic reform. In the first instance, this meant joining the defence organisation NATO. In the spring and summer of 1997, he went on a tour of Europe's capitals to promote the idea and seek support for Romania's application. It wasn't successful, but he found himself *persona grata* again, and Romania was eventually admitted to NATO on its second application in 2004. The trickier task was the European Union, because almost every aspect of democratic and civilised life in Romania had been devastated by half a century of the most unrelenting totalitarian regime in Europe. But even there, Romania has prevailed, joining the EU in 2007.

Michael died in December 2017, a little over ninety years after he first became King of Romania. He dedicated his life to standing up for the constitutional rights of his people, for their civilisation and for their place in Europe. And he did so, almost uniquely, during the bad years, when so many other Romanians succumbed to pressure from the regime, to a financial offer from the CIA, or to the many distractions available in exile. The result was a unique moral authority, which received such a rapturous reception in 1992 and which twenty years later still made him the most trusted political figure in Romania. And where he led, others have followed, although almost certainly not consciously. Today, numerous Ex Men are using their years after office to speak up against successor governments, not on narrow political grounds but on the basis that they are undermining democracy, rolling back constitutional rights or diminishing their nations' standing in the world. Others, while hardly paragons of virtue themselves, nevertheless hold firm for some basic democratic standards, and if not that then at least some basic competence in government. They have run countries as varied as Turkey, Poland, Thailand and Malaysia, and they really matter.

• • •

'The new President is arguing that Turkey needs a stronger presidency. Is this healthy? Is this good for Turkey, to have a stronger presidency than you had when you were President?'

'I have stated my feelings about this when I was in Turkey. If you allow me, I'm not going to add to them.'

'But we didn't hear them, and they were in Turkish. You couldn't say them for our translator? Was it a very simple "good as it is" or "things are fine as they are"?'

'I said this openly in Turkey … Everyone knows that I see a parliamentary system as a better, more suitable system. But of course, one cannot say that a presidential system is not a good system. For example, how can you say the United States is not a democracy, is not a suitable, proper regime? But to be able to have that sort of a presidential regime, you need to check everything. You need to have your balances in the right place etc.'

It's November 2014 and a newly minted Ex Man, the very recent President of Turkey, is answering questions at the Chatham House think tank in London. Abdullah Gül has spent close to an hour answering questions but it's the very last one which intrigues me. His long-time ally Recep Tayyip Erdoğan, with whom he co-founded Turkey's ruling Justice and Development Party (AKP), has just succeeded him, and there are rumours that Erdoğan would like to do away with Turkey's parliamentary system and concentrate powers in the presidency. And Gül, while clearly uncomfortable with it, appears even more uncomfortable answering questions about it. Six months later, his reservations seemed to be slipping as he spoke more directly of the importance of those checks and balances; six months after that and he was stressing again the importance of diversity and different voices in an interview with the *Financial Times*.[3]

In the years since, Erdoğan has brushed aside Gül's concerns and transformed the Turkish presidency. Those changes, together with emergency legislation and a populist turn after a 2016 coup attempt, led Freedom House, an American think tank which scores countries' democratic institutions, to downgrade Turkey to a country which is 'not free'. Gül has clearly struggled with the changes and continues to speak out, warning about decrees, criticising populism, disapproving of the dismissal of opposition mayors, calling for greater freedom, arguing that the country's relations with the West are 'off balance'.[4] What he hasn't done, though, is challenge Erdoğan directly, by forming or joining a new party. There have been repeated rumours that he might: in one interview in December 2016 he said he'd been asked the question forty times.[5] But he has shown little interest in defecting, repeatedly distancing himself from the rumours. And then in 2019, the time suddenly seemed right. The AKP was soundly defeated in a set of local elections, and the rumour mill started up again: Gül had defected, he would soon form a new political party.[6] Later that year, his fellow Turkish Ex Man, former Prime Minister Ahmet Davutoğlu, did make the leap and set up a new party. But as summer turned to autumn, and still Gül remained silent, it became clear that he would not, in fact, be challenging Erdoğan.[7] His struggle – between his fidelity to the founding principles of the AKP, his belief in Turkish democratic and civic institutions, and his oft-stated wish to retreat from public life – illustrates the difficulties Ex Men can face when seeking to follow King Michael's example. It must be particularly difficult when it involves a break from allies, rather than opponents. Once you've made the break, though, like Lech Wałęsa in Poland, it can deepen quite fast. Wałęsa was the communist-era leader of the trade union Solidarity who won the Nobel Peace Prize en route to becoming his country's first democratically elected President. His 2006 falling out with erstwhile allies the Kaczyński brothers and their Law and Justice Party (PiS) has turned into a deep and permanent rift. When PiS attempted to reform Poland's judiciary, he joined protests, asked the European Union to intervene and took to wearing a T-shirt emblazoned with the word 'Konstytucja' (meaning 'Constitution'). He seems to wear little else: onstage, outside, and even to the state funeral of his friend and former US President George H. W. Bush. A friend to whom I showed the photo asked if it wasn't disrespectful, but if the idea is to protest in the strongest possible way, where better to do it than in front of the largest possible audience? And then, in April 2020, Wałęsa joined many of his fellow Polish Ex Men in urging a boycott of what they called Poland's presidential 'pseudo election', held in the middle of the coronavirus pandemic, and which duly produced a PiS victory.

• • •

Gül and Wałęsa have lent their moral voices to political arguments, but in other countries Ex Men continue to have an outsize sway in criticising their successors' perceived transgressions, too, both political and managerial. When I asked former Nigerian President Olusegun Obasanjo about this back in 2015, it was just a few weeks after I'd seen him at the Royal African Society in London. There, to loud cheers of laughter and support on the one hand, and derision on the other, he had laid into the sitting President Goodluck Jonathan in typically colourful terms. 'I've been a little bit active at home, which some people try to run away from, and I believe that it's obligatory on the part of us leaders who, when we see things going wrong, we must have the conviction to go out and, if necessary, stick out our neck,' he told me. 'You shouldn't be doing that all the time of course. Like they say, a dog that barks all the time will be irrelevant, and a dog that doesn't bark at all is as useless as not having a dog.'

Obasanjo, a powerful figure in Nigerian politics for almost forty-five years, is certainly not afraid to bark, but since serving his final term as President he has remained out of elective politics. In Thailand, the former Prime Minister and businessman who at one time owned Manchester City Football Club, Thaksin Shinawatra, has also remained out of elective politics since leaving office, but for very different reasons. Deposed in a 2006 military coup after months of street protests, Thaksin has lived in exile since, but the various incarnations of his party have won every open election since then, leading to another military coup in 2014, when his younger sister Yingluck Shinawatra, then the Prime Minister, was also turfed out of office. Thaksin was Thailand's first modern Prime Minister, and his appeal to ordinary Thai voters in the north of the country, and willingness to make good on promises to provide them with healthcare and financial support, represented a challenge to traditional elites. As such, despite living out of office and in exile for almost twenty-five years, he remains a significant figure in Thai politics.

In neighbouring Malaysia, meanwhile, Mahathir Mohamad has

been a central figure for almost exactly as long as Obasanjo has pulled the strings in Nigeria. Prime Minister for more than twenty years, Mahathir was the dominant figure, on one hand creating modern Malaysia while on the other courting controversy for his scepticism about civil liberties and willingness to wield power, including against his Deputy Prime Minister Anwar Ibrahim, who ended up in prison. When he eventually retired after twenty-two years as Prime Minister, Mahathir found the temptation to meddle too hard to resist: instrumental in the downfall of his hand-picked successor, he gained a reputation as a 'kingmaker and kingslayer'. And then, for a while, he was quiet. But in 2015, a scandal erupted involving then Prime Minister Najib Razak. Najib was accused of diverting hundreds of millions of dollars of money from 1MDB, a government-run strategic development company, into his private accounts, and Mahathir spoke up, urging him to resign. Over the course of the next three years, Najib dug in and Mahathir became increasingly outspoken: he called for a public uprising, lost a government-sanctioned advisory role, was investigated by the police, and sued the Prime Minister. Eventually Anwar Ibrahim, now the opposition leader, sent word from his jail cell that he would lend Mahathir his support. The men met and shook hands, and in January 2018 Mahathir Mohamad, aged ninety-two, was nominated by the opposition alliance as their candidate for Prime Minister, winning the election and serving a little under two years, eventually retiring for the second time just shy of his ninety-fifth birthday. Even then, the saga continued: his successor as Prime Minister pulled out of one governing coalition to form another and dumped Mohamad out of the party.

For his part, Najib Razak's induction into the Ex Men's guild has been rather less than delightful. Prosecution and conviction followed investigation and in July 2020 he was sentenced to twelve years in prison after being found guilty on seven charges (he plans to appeal). It's a familiar development over the past two decades. Where once a former President or Prime Minister with a questionable human rights record or who is surprisingly wealthy after a lifetime spent in political offices with very low official salaries might have been able quietly to slink away and spend their money in peace, today they're just as likely to find themselves, like Najib, on the wrong end of a fraud conviction. Whether it's Romania, Italy, Israel, Pakistan or South Africa, Ex Men are under the microscope; one study suggested that between 1990 and 2008, sixty-seven heads of government were criminally charged for misconduct.[8] South Korea has had it especially bad: every living former President except one has been convicted and sentenced to jail; another committed suicide while under investigation. In Latin America, investigations into the octopus-like Odebrecht scandal have ensnared multiple Ex Men and sitting Presidents alike in allegations of corruption running into the tens of millions of dollars (although those accused have denied any wrongdoing). But it's in Peru where this unhappy history reaches its nadir, a nadir deeper even than the suicide of former President Alan García, who killed himself when police tried to arrest him as part of the Odebrecht investigation. No, this goes back further, to the summer of 1990.

That year's presidential election campaign saw a battle between two political heavyweights: Luis Alva Castro, the former Prime Minister and candidate of Peru's governing APRA Party, and Mario Vargas Llosa, the celebrated writer and future Nobel Prize winner. Except neither really caught on with Peruvian voters; instead, in the waning weeks of the campaign, a dark-horse candidate, a little-known former university professor running with few promises except that he'd bring change, suddenly emerged as a real threat to both men. Alberto Fujimori won the election, and with Peru's run-away inflation and a decade of brutal insurgency from the Shining Path guerrillas which had wreaked havoc on its social, economic and cultural fabric, it was clear to anyone why his message of change had struck such a chord. Less clear was what he was going to do about either problem, but ten years later, the unheralded Fujimori had defeated the insurgency and put Peru on a more sustainable economic path. Peruvians had seen the change, but Fujimori's remedies had been brutal. In November 2000, amid mounting uproar over a corruption scandal, he fled the country, eventually submitting his resignation – by fax – from Japan. Over the next several years he was investigated not just over allegations of corruption but over serious human rights abuses. Finally arrested on a visit to Chile, he was extradited to Peru, charged, tried, convicted and imprisoned. Fujimori's family and political allies tried to get him released, of course, but the only legal remedy was a presidential pardon, available only on narrow and specific humanitarian grounds. In 2012, they requested just such a pardon, which was rejected.

And that might have been the end of the story, except that during Fujimori's presidency his daughter, Keiko, had acquired a taste for political life. After his imprisonment she entered politics herself, founded a political party and ran twice for President, losing by quite a large margin in 2011 and then again by a very narrow margin in 2016. That, too, is another moment when this story might have ended; where Fujimori's personal tragedy might have naturally de-coupled from Peru's national story. Except that it didn't then, either.

Eighteen months on and the man who won the 2016 election, President Pedro Pablo Kuczynski, was in trouble. Deeply unpop-ular and himself mired in the Odebrecht scandal, he faced an impeachment vote in Peru's Parliament. With the enthusiastic support of opposition MPs in Keiko Fujimori's Popular Force Party, the motion seemed certain to pass; Kuczynski's days were numbered. And then, at the very last moment, a young Popular Force MP led a breakaway group opposing the impeachment. Kuczynski narrowly survived and three days later, on Christmas Eve, he pardoned Fujimori. The young MP who had backed him? Fujimori's son, Keiji. Cue: uproar. Protesters took to the streets, the international human rights community exploded, and members of Kuczynski's government resigned. The widely held assumption was that in issuing the pardon, Kuczynski was rewarding Keiji Fujimori. Three months later, and in the throes of a second impeachment process, President Kuczynski eventually resigned. The elder Fujimori himself was released and then, when the pardon was eventually overturned, returned to prison. The whole tale reads rather like a negative mirror image of King Michael's story; an extraordinary tale of the corrupting power of an Ex Man. But it's not the only one. Nor, sadly, the worst.

• • •

'Taylor's most important ploy for demonstrating and solidifying power … was his use of violence,' wrote the west African expert and anthropologist David Hoffman of former Liberian President Charles Taylor.[9] A brutal strongman during the Liberian civil war, Taylor won power in the 1997 general election and ruled, according to Hoffman, 'through control over the trade in resources and the "cultural capital" accrued through his ability to manipulate violence and the dramaturgy of power'.[10] In practical terms, that meant a shrewd understanding of how to use propaganda as a threat: on the one hand, extreme violence; on the other, T-shirts printed with images of him meeting with Jimmy Carter. Look, he's saying to Liberians: this is what I can do to you, and this is why you can't touch me. They couldn't, of course, but they were fortunate, in a sense, that Taylor's reign of terror happened in the early part of the twenty-first century, and not a decade or two earlier. It meant there was a chance that Taylor's atrocities would eventually catch up with him, and in 2003 they did. After much cajoling, including by a Who's Who of African Presidents, Taylor was persuaded to leave office and go into a comfortable exile in Nigeria. At least he's not still in power, a destabilising force for the whole region, went the reasoning, but it was a bitter pill for his victims to see him in exile, apparently protected from justice. And what's more, he remained a destabilising presence.

Taylor's example is an extreme case of the difficulty of balancing transitional justice and the requirements of political stability, but it is far from the only one. This balance was a concern in many of the sixty-seven cases of Ex Men charged with misconduct in that 2008 study, and in many cases since then, although perhaps fewer as time goes on. As the authors of that study wrote, 'The issue was no longer whether there should be accountability, but how much and what kind of accountability, as well as what compromises were acceptable to keep the peace or prevent a return to authoritarian rule.'[11] Since many of the newer cases are less about transitions from authoritarian rule and more about abuses within an existing democratic system, fewer instances call for this intricate balancing act, which needs to balance trials 'with other democratic transition priorities such as maintaining order, placating a restive military or other armed fighters (especially those loyal to a potential defendant), demobilizing and reintegrating ex-combatants, or staving off economic collapse'.[12] Even if more cases are now within existing democratic systems rather than transitions from authoritarian rule, recent improvements in national and international justice systems, such that so many Ex Men now find themselves under criminal investigation, might make it harder than ever to persuade truly nefarious rulers to step aside.

In Charles Taylor's case, his presence eventually became too destabilising, tipping the balance in favour of justice. Three years after his exile, and with a democratic government installed in Liberia, its new President, Ellen Johnson Sirleaf, requested his extradition. He was sent for trial by the international Special Court for Sierra Leone, found guilty on eleven counts of aiding and abetting war crimes and crimes against humanity, including terrorism, rape and murder, use of child soldiers and enslavement, and sentenced to fifty years in prison.

His case is a reminder of the powerful hold which some Ex Men continue to have over their nations – for good and ill. But there are some Ex Men who continue to have a hold over more than just their nation.

CHAPTER 8

BRAND EX

It's a Sunday night in early November 2012. Despite the bitter cold and the fact that it's fast approaching midnight, 20,000 people are crammed into a music venue in the suburbs of northern Virginia, about an hour's drive outside Washington DC. As they huddle together for warmth, the singer Dave Matthews entertains them with some of his hits and, this being the weekend before the presidential election, some political chat. Matthews is a big enough star that even those in the audience who don't quite know who he is recognise the songs. He's headlined much larger venues than this before, but tonight he seems happy to take his place in the long roster, a warm-up to the warm-up. As he leaves the stage to enthusiastic applause, a frisson runs through the crowd, and the first of a series of Mexican waves wends its way around the arena, peters out as it reaches the stage, and gathers pace again as it arrives back at the expectant crowd. In a little over an hour this huge audience will get to see the man whose name is on their tickets, their wristbands and their posters when the main act strides out on stage and asks the crowd to give him four more years as President of the United States.

Tonight, Barack Obama is energised. After months of debating, speechifying and hand-shaking, gone is the languor which has sometimes marred his re-election campaign. In its place is a punchiness, a fiery populism which only occasionally veers off into well-meaning policy wonkery. When it does, he loses the crowd and the energy in the stadium begins to dip, but he knows enough by now, at the end of his last run for public office, to be able to recover it. And so, in sub-zero temperatures and at the end of a campaign where he has often failed to light the fires of the faithful, there is tremendous, and genuine, warmth for Obama here tonight. As he runs through his various achievements, his hopes for the next four years, and his opposition to every plank of the Republican platform, the crowd whoop and holler their support. But despite their admiration, the crowd here haven't saved their loudest applause for President Obama's stump speech. For tonight there is someone on the bill who really tugs at Democratic heartstrings, someone this crowd really respond to. And watching them rally to the call from Obama's warm-up man, an ageing, silver-haired baby boomer who had almost lost his voice, it's clear he can reach and stir something in the audience that Obama just can't. It's been a remarkable campaign for him, stepping in to help refine Obama's message and in the process define the younger man's legacy. Even more remarkable, he hasn't held government office for twelve years; when last he did, his personal failures brought him and the country to the brink of disaster; and the last campaign he helped run – against, of all people, Barack Obama – ended in failure. They know all this, but still the crowd can't get enough of Bill Clinton.

And nor can anyone else. Since he left office in something approaching disgrace, Clinton has rebuilt his reputation, enhanced his brand and launched an extraordinary assault on every problem he thinks he might be of some assistance in solving, from the availability of HIV medicine in sub-Saharan Africa to childhood obesity in the United States. His Clinton Foundation is like a little

White House on the Hudson, churning out ideas and initiatives, a centre for leaders from around the world to meet, discuss and act. His Clinton Global Initiative has become the hottest ticket in global philanthropy, with billionaires and major corporations lining up to promise good deeds (and with the sword of Damocles – not being invited back – hanging over them if they don't deliver). And all this while he has built an almost filial relationship with the presidential predecessor he defeated and an almost fraternal relationship with the successor who demonised him.

•   •   •

Some of that is still true in 2020, but it doesn't feel the same. Clinton is still a magnetic speaker and he can still attract a crowd, but the shine is definitely off. And while the change in Bill Clinton's fortunes is far from the most striking thing to happen in politics since that cold November night eight years ago, it is striking. It's the result in part of a reconsideration, post-#MeToo, of his relationships with women. Partly it's his widely reported missteps in his wife's two presidential campaigns, and her two defeats, particularly in 2016. And partly it's down to the operation of the Clinton Foundation – such a boon for a former President raising money and using his contacts and visibility on behalf of worthy causes; such a bane for a potential President when journalists and political adversaries started noting the political debts which might be owed to foreign governments.

When Bill Clinton left office, he was just fifty-four years old, the most naturally gifted politician of his generation, and better connected than any other human being on the planet. He was also in enormous debt; his wife, whom he had deeply embarrassed during the Lewinsky scandal just three years earlier, had just been elected a senator from New York State; and a pardon he had issued to the fugitive financier Marc Rich had engulfed him in another scandal on his way out of the White House. Clinton looked around for what he could do next, and in Jimmy Carter he saw a model for his own post-presidency. 'I just love the fact that he never stopped learning, never stopped taking on challenges,' Clinton told David Remnick of the *New Yorker* in 2006, 'and I wanted to talk to him about it, because I thought his foundation was as close as anybody had come to kinda what I wanted to do.'[1] And so, just like Carter twenty years earlier, Clinton started developing programmes and projects and hasn't stopped since. He hasn't got his hands dirty in the way Carter has, of course – no one else has – but he has worked hard for the causes he espouses. Like Tony Blair, he's also become a rich man during the process; like Tony Blair, there are questions about how – and from whom – some of that money has been raised. But there is no question that a lot of his initiatives have had a real impact. Two, in particular, stand out. His HIV/AIDS procurement consortium, established at a time when HIV was rampaging across Africa and governments seemed like rabbits in headlights, dazzled by the scale of the health crisis unfolding, the speed with which it was spreading, and the price of the drugs to help ease the suffering. Enter Bill Clinton, using his convening power and astonishing network to cajole drug companies into reducing prices, enabling donors and developing countries to commit to buying them, in turn, at enormous scale. Its success has transformed millions of lives. And second, the Clinton Global Initiative. Girls Not Brides was just one of more than 3,600 commitments made in its eleven-year existence. Clinton's website claims today that those commitments have improved the lives of 435 million people in more than 180 countries, and while it's unlikely anyone will get into the weeds of every last one to tot up its exact impact, they were designed to be measurable. And not just that: new, specific, viable and accountable were the other thresholds a commitment had to meet.

But Clinton's empire has not been without its share of controversy, notably during Hillary Clinton's presidential runs. After all, where a multi-million-dollar donation from a foreign government might look fine if you're very much an Ex Man, a former President in Jimmy Carter's mould operating independently of government, it might look very different if your wife is in government, as Secretary of State – or President. Then, perhaps, it might look more like a debt; like an IOU which can be called upon at a tricky moment. In 2008, the people around President Obama were sufficiently worried about this perception that they ensured Hillary Clinton's appointment as Secretary of State was accompanied by a careful study of the Clinton Foundation's finances and guarantees of future standards.[2] In 2016, it was just one of the sticks Donald Trump used to beat the Clintons.

Optics aside, over the years Clinton's portfolio of projects has included many of the other roles I've described in this book. He's been an advocate; by all accounts a very effective one. He's run projects on all kinds of issues. He's been a prolific fundraiser: on his own behalf, on behalf of his foundation and, at the request of President George W. Bush, on behalf of charities dealing with terrible natural disasters. This role led to a strange, not-quite-sibling relationship with President Bush, and even stranger, not-quite-son relationship with Bush's father, George H. W. Bush, with whom he raised funds on behalf of the victims of the 2004 Indian Ocean tsunami, and later Hurricane Katrina. As one commentator noted, 'the two Presidents whose two most famous quotes were untrue – "read my lips" and "I did not have sexual relations with that woman" – were now so trusted that Americans who wanted to help hurricane victims were simply sending Bush and Clinton cash'.[3] But he made it work, and there seemed genuine warmth from both parties in those relationships. Clinton has even held international jobs, appointed in 2009 as UN Special Envoy to Haiti after the country's devastating earthquake and another marathon fundraiser, this time with (now former) President George W. Bush. The fundraiser went well, but not every part of Clinton's engagement was a stunning success. About a year into his job as UN Special Envoy, I asked Michèle Pierre-Louis, Haiti's Prime Minister when he was appointed, what she made of his tenure. She'd seen the benefits of his involvement, she told me, but she also noted the growing criticism of the Interim Haiti Recovery Commission, which Clinton co-chaired.

> There is still some criticism about the Interim Commission in Haiti, saying that they're not doing enough. But at the same time, I don't want to be too critical myself … President Clinton will continue to be there, be involved and be engaged, and talk about Haiti, which is a good thing.

I'd heard some rumours that Clinton appeared more concerned about preserving his legacy than with rebuilding the country – and when I put them to her, Pierre-Louis spoke slowly and chose her words carefully. 'President Clinton is a star, so I suppose he's always concerned about his stardom,' she said, and then paused. 'It's our responsibility, as Haitians, not only to stand up for what we want, but to design, with President Clinton, the role that he can play in Haiti.' Another pause. 'If we haven't done that, it gives him the leeway to just be charming,' she concluded, laughing.

Bill Clinton has continued in that vein, although perhaps the

#MeToo movement has caused some to reassess how charming some of that charm really was. And as he ages, he seems to have slowed down. But he remains a huge draw: his Clinton Global Initiative University event in 2020 was sufficiently attractive to persuade New York State Governor Andrew Cuomo and California Governor Gavin Newsom to step away from dealing with the Covid-19 pandemic and speak to him. And of course, as with Tony Blair's post-premiership, Clinton's post-presidency sustains a minor publishing industry all of its own.[4] It's a reflection of his stature; that he is, in the words of one ally, 'a brand, a world-wide brand, and he can do things and ask for things that no one else can.'[5] A Brand Ex, if you will.

•   •   •

And what of those others who are big enough, famous enough, energetic enough, to be a Brand Ex? I think there are just three of them, one who already redefined what it is to be an Ex Man, and two who have the potential to do so. The first, and the biggest Brand Ex of recent years, was former South African President Nelson Mandela. His post-presidency, according to one observer, was a continuation by other means of his premiership. 'With barely a pause,' observed John Daniel, 'the now former president just kept on pursuing those issues and goals which had preoccupied him throughout his five-year presidency, but which he had pursued most particularly in the last three years of his term.'[6] Most important, Daniel argues, was his work on HIV/AIDS. Mandela's successor, Thabo Mbeki, was a prominent sceptic of the scientific consensus that HIV caused AIDS, pursuing policies to limit the use of drugs which controlled HIV and helped prevent its transmission.

Mandela spoke out, first privately and eventually publicly, against this denialism, meeting prominent activists and legitimising what they were saying. This engagement, like the Latin American Commission on Drugs and Democracy, eventually began to turn the tide of public opinion against the government's position. And of course it wasn't just any former President speaking out but South Africa's revered secular saint. Later, when he took that same moral stature and invested it elsewhere, speaking out, for example, against the war in Iraq, Daniel argues that it had a similar effect, creating space for legitimate criticism of the rush to war. 'To his public it mattered not one bit whether it was President or former President Mandela speaking – what he said (and did) carried weight and authority, irrespective of his office or status,' Daniel concludes.[7] I'm sure he's right about the moral stature, but I can't help thinking that former prisoner Mandela, however morally powerful, would have carried a lot less weight than former President Mandela.

And then there are the other two, the two men who last year shared the honour of being named the most admired men in America: Barack Obama and Donald Trump.[8] One, of course, is not yet an Ex Man, and may not be until 2025; the other has spent most of the past four years enjoying his freedom, writing his memoirs and raising money for his presidential library, with only a few hints about what he might do afterwards. There's a tradition in the Ex-Presidents' Club that they don't criticise their successors, but 2020 is a testing time, and by the time this book is published we will know whether that tradition can survive the fracturing of American political life.[9] And beyond that, what will Obama do? He and his wife Michelle have signed an agreement to produce shows and films for Netflix, but surely that won't be enough to sate his intellectual curiosity and his wish to do good in the world? Perhaps the examples in this book offer food for thought. Any of the options would be open to him: most international organisations, NGOs, diplomatic initiatives or members' clubs would be delighted to have him involved. If he wants to be effective, the calculation is a rather different one. Carter, Clinton, Mandela and Blair all offer slightly different lessons. Carter's is perhaps the satisfaction which can come from choosing untrendy, offbeat topics, making them your own and achieving something special. From Clinton, it's the power of personality – and contacts – to persuade others to make the best of themselves. From Mandela, the moral voice. And sadly from Blair, whatever the upside to his work with emerging African democracies, the lesson best learned is the damage to your efficacy caused by no longer caring about your public image.

What a different story it will be for Obama's successor, Donald Trump. Part of my argument in this book is that the current crop of Ex Men made the modern world we live in today: liberal, globalised, democratic, and that they continue to advocate for those values once they leave office. But Trump won't. Trump doesn't believe in globalisation in the way that his predecessors did; in important respects, his understanding of democracy, and of liberalism, are different too. The journalist and historian Kate Andersen Brower explained recently how challenging it will be for Trump to be accepted into the Ex-Presidents' Club. In an interview, he told her he didn't expect to attend the opening of Barack Obama's library, for example. 'He probably wouldn't invite me,' Trump explained to her, before mulling it a moment and asking, 'Why should he?'[10] Perhaps he'll be content to retreat from public life, in the model of the two Presidents Bush, but that doesn't look especially likely, does it? And so what will he do? I think the lesson of this book is clear: his style and political positions make him an outlier amongst Ex

Men, and few if any of the opportunities open to Obama will be open to Trump – few international organisations, NGOs, diplomatic initiatives or members' clubs would want him involved. That's not to say nobody would, but this book is about Ex Men who achieve things after office, and without any of the institutional infrastructure it's hard to create meaningful change. In fact, it's hard to create meaningful change even *with* the institutional infrastructure. But don't bet against him. Lots of people did in 2016. And he humiliated them.

CHAPTER 9

THE LAST STAND

'I received a visit from the armed forces that said that they would not support my presidency any more.' Former President of Ecuador Jamil Mahuad is telling me about the coup that toppled his government. 'I said, "It is my duty to be here at the presidential palace," and I made a broadcast saying, "I will not resign."' We're at an upscale restaurant just outside Boston, and the juxtaposition of fancy table service and this extraordinary story is jarring. 'Then I received news that the armed forces would not guarantee my security, and I still thought, "That is the risk of being President that comes with the territory," and decided to stay there.' Mahuad pauses.

My military aide and the people he commanded said it is part of the military code that they would never allow that to happen, even at the cost of their lives. Later, the military commanders sent me the message that they could not guarantee the security of the civil servants in the presidential palace, and that was in my view something I could not morally afford. I could make any decision with my life, but how could I put in danger the lives of civil servants? So at that point in time I decided to leave the presidential palace, and for the first time in my presidency they invited me to use a bulletproof vest.

Mahuad and his aides went to Quito airport, where he again refused to smooth the path for the coup leaders by resigning and
instead challenged them to overthrow him properly. 'The junta that
was formed in the morning couldn't consolidate as a government,'
Mahuad continues.

> I was at the airport until 10 or 11 p.m., and then we had a new
> TV broadcast from the presidential palace where another junta
> was formed, and at that point they were saying, 'We are the new
> government of Ecuador,' they were giving press conferences and
> interviews.

Mahuad had been elected to office only eighteen months earlier,
just as a perfect storm of agricultural shortages, extreme weather
and severe economic problems hit a country ill-prepared for any
of them, let alone all three. By the time of the coup, this Harvard-
trained technocrat had tried everything he could to fix them, to
little avail. And so here he was, in the middle of the night, at the
airport, in the middle of a coup, and it was anyone's guess which
way it would turn out. So Mahuad travelled back into the city,
awakening the next morning to a phone call telling him to turn on
the TV. 'And on the TV was my Vice-President taking office, and
the Congress was convened to bless all that.' Now it *was* clear what
was happening, and after calling on the public to support the new
government in the difficult days ahead, Mahuad decided that it was
time to leave the country. He travelled first to Peru and Chile, and
then Harvard invited him back to develop a lecture series about the
crises he had faced during his presidency. Ten years later, here he
is, still talking about the crises, only this time over breakfast, with
me. Beyond the alumni connection, there's another reason Harvard

was happy to host Mahuad, and it's the reason he's still here today. It's about the Ecuadorian crisis Mahuad was able to resolve. 'When we signed the peace treaty with Peru, President Clinton said, "You have solved the oldest source of armed conflict in this hemisphere,"' Mahuad tells me. 'The Peru–Ecuador border line dispute was on the list of intractable problems in the world. We had wars every ten, twelve, fifteen years. All the odds were against any possible solution.' Except, and with another war looming, just five years after the last one, Mahuad did just that. If ever there were a happy ending to a story, resolving a hundreds-of-years-old border dispute is surely it. But the ending for the Presidents on both sides was decidedly less happy. In Mahuad's case, his inglorious departure mattered less to universities than his achievement in that historic peace deal, and it has allowed him to burnish his legacy and create a new life for himself. As for his Peruvian counterpart, Alberto Fujimori – well, as we know, his post-presidency took a far darker turn. It's the starkest possible reminder that an Ex Man's career will be defined by their conduct in office and by the manner of their departure. I'm reminded of former Czech President Václav Havel's comments on Mikhail Gorbachev, from his marvellous, off-the-wall memoir. 'He is a special and, in his own way, a tragic case,' Havel writes.

> He tried to lift up the lid to let some of the steam out of the pot, and it clearly never occurred to him that a lid, once lifted, can – and, given the magnitude of the pressure, must – be blown away forever. His historical achievement is enormous: communism would have collapsed without him anyway, but it might have happened ten years later, and in God knows how wild and bloody a fashion. Nevertheless, for obvious reasons, this type of achievement does not and cannot entitle him to play an active political

role in entirely new circumstances, particularly when those circumstances were not something he sought in the first place.[1]

This final chapter, then, is about how Ex Men preserve their legacies.
It's about their books, their libraries and the other institutions they
use to protect and project power; about their lives on the speech
circuit; and about how they survive, financially and emotionally,
and the harm that can do.

• • •

'I heard the Downing Street switchboard say to Mr Blair, "Prime Minister, I have Mr Major on the line."'[2] John Major was still Prime Minister when he placed that call, to concede the election and congratulate
his successor. It was 2 a.m. and while millions of votes had still to be
counted, it was clear to all that he would soon be joining the ranks of
the Ex Men. Such is the brutal transition of power in Britain, but least
he'd been turned out of office by voters. For Jim Bolger, the transition
to Ex Man was made a lot harder because it was party colleagues who
turned on him. 'There is absolute hurt, when people that you've pro-
moted, guided and assisted through their political lives all of a sudden
turn on you,' he says. 'Of course it's hurtful when they decide, without
consultation, that you're past your use-by date.' And remember how
Jack McConnell, the former First Minister of Scotland, changed the
start-up message on his mobile phone so it read 'lucky, not unlucky'?
It helped counter his feelings of frustration, mourning the creative
working environment he had lost and the political impotence he felt,
no longer able to solve problems on a grand scale. The unexpected-
ness and brutality of these transitions, the vanished hope that perhaps
they might get to keep the job they loved, made it all the harder. But

in the United States, planning for the transition to the presidential afterlife begins long before leaving office.

•   •   •

It's June 1998 and at the end of a year studying in America a friend and I have decided to drive together across the country, from Boston in the east to Oakland in the west, where she has a summer job. Traditionally there are two routes – a northern route, through Chicago and the great plains, or a southern route, through the great southern cities. But Hilary and I have chosen a middle route, because I want to visit two small towns in Kansas and Missouri, to visit the presidential libraries and museums of Dwight Eisenhower in Abilene, Kansas; and Harry Truman in Independence, Missouri. We duly make these pilgrimages, nearly getting blown off the road by a tornado on our way out of Kansas; later in the trip I visit the Richard Nixon Library in California and the Lyndon B. Johnson Library in Texas. Since then I've had the pleasure of doing research there, and in the John F. Kennedy library in Boston, as well as visiting the libraries and museums of Jimmy Carter in Atlanta, Georgia; and of the two Presidents Bush, both in Texas. I love these libraries, where Presidents send their papers and other records accumulated during their time in office so that they can be pored over by historians; and I love their museums, where Presidents tell the story about themselves that they'd like the world to know. 'It is safe to assume that visitors receive only a positive perspective toward an administration,' presidential scholar Richard Spears wrote of the museums, noting the regular disjuncture between the museum and the accompanying library: 'Two stories are being told: one by the document collection and the other by the exhibits.'[3] I think that's what makes them fascinating, and over time you can watch as the stories being told gradually move closer together.

These institutions may be the grandest physical incarnation of the post-presidential drive to define an Ex Man's own legacy, but they are far from the only ones, and perhaps not even the most influential. That, surely, is the memoir, described by presidential historian Douglas Brinkley as 'among the worst of all literary genres', due to their inauthenticity.[4] I'm not so sure. I've read a lot of them, and as a result I have read a lot of drivel. But I've also read some excellent books. I think Fernando Henrique Cardoso's book, which also offers a history of modern Brazil, is a fascinating read; George H. W. Bush's memoir, co-written with his erstwhile National Security Advisor Brent Scowcroft, is a stunning portrait of the decision-making process inside the White House at the end of the Cold War, all the more powerful because of the way each man describes the events from his perspective, sometimes disagreeing along the way.[5] Most, though, are more run-of-the-mill efforts to manage their legacies, to tell their stories, explain their motivations, perhaps even settle a score or two. As Kim Campbell puts it, 'I wanted people to know who I was.' And besides reading a lot of the books, I've also had an opportunity to speak to a lot of their authors about them. Until I did, I assumed they were mainly a way to manage that legacy, to find something concrete to do after leaving office, and to raise some money. That is without a doubt a central part of it. David Cameron was so concerned about the content of his memoirs that he asked a friend, journalist Daniel Finkelstein, to come and speak to him regularly throughout his premiership, recording their conversations, so that he would have an accurate record of his thinking about what was going on. How's that for legacy management? But that conversation with Kim Campbell, quite early on in the research for this book, gave me a perspective beyond this. 'I think the memoir may have helped clarify in my own mind, or remind me, really, who I was, to help sort through all the dross and confusion of events at the time and look back at a broader thematic framework of my life,' she told me. This puts a very different spin on telling the world who she was; she first had to find out herself.

> I don't think I put the pen down and said, 'Well, it's clear now what I must do,' but really more that I was surprised. 'My goodness, there is a rhyme or reason to my life, it wasn't always accidental or higgledy-piggledy. The choices I made were very consistent throughout my life.

Just as important, she told me that she thought that same narrative was reflected in her life since leaving office. And once Kim Campbell told me that, I began wondering how many Ex Men may, like her, never previously have sat back and taken stock of their lives. In particular, for those with less ideological dispositions it may be the first time they identify a single story or narrative about the decisions they have taken.

Even for those with a very clear, consistent or unflinching attach-ment to some issue or idea, like Mary Robinson, writing the book can be important in helping to tell that story or highlighting some critical moment. So the memoir in this reading is legacy manage-ment and therapy at the same time, an opportunity to clarify or remind them of who they really are.

Of course, memoirs also help earn money. Sometimes lots of it. The bidding for David Cameron's memoirs reached £800,000, a sharp drop from the £4.6 million Tony Blair is reported to have earned just a few years earlier, but still an enormous sum.* From a

---

* Blair donated the advance and all his proceeds from the book to the Royal British Legion.

commercial perspective, books should hit the bookshops as soon as possible, according to Stuart Proffitt, who published both Margaret Thatcher's and John Major's literary endeavours. He told BBC Radio 4's Michael Crick that the key ingredients are 'candour, newsworthiness, readability, authenticity, a willingness to admit mistakes, say what you really think. That's what the public want to know.'[6] Over time, the venom and vitriol exhibited by authors has waxed and waned, although the furore in Australia over the recent publication of former PM Malcolm Turnbull's memoirs suggests that there is plenty of appetite for score-settling. But what of the other forms of what has been called 'remunerative reminiscence'?[7]

•   •   •

'Broadly, for someone like Cameron, in China, you'd be looking at something around $150,000.' Per speech? 'Mmm.' For one speech? 'China's got a lot of money.' Evidently, but who thinks David Cameron is good value at $150,000? 'They don't, but British Prime Minister is the strapline. The Chinese are obsessed by number ones. You can't sell them the number two.' So Theresa May? 'Number one!' She'd do well, would she? 'Yes, no problem.' Is she worth $150,000 a time? 'You have to feel it's basically in the same area. There isn't a judgement on performance. She is new on the scene, so there is a premium. She's female, she's had a very challenging premiership, which a lot of the world have picked up on.' In his office in west London, Tom Kenyon-Slaney is giving me a primer on how to market Ex Men as public speakers. He founded and still runs the London Speaker Bureau, one of the world's largest speaker agencies, with offices in every major market. Having read the papers over the years, I know that Ex Men can command exorbitant fees for a single speech, but still I'm amazed by this focus on the office, not the record. Theresa May is only a month out of office, and she conspicuously failed in the central task she set herself during her premiership: getting Brexit done. So can he be serious? 'It's irrelevant who the person is, when you're talking Prime Minister level, President level...' He can, apparently.

> I look after [former French President] François Hollande. Now, if you go to the French business community, they'll say, 'God, terrible.' And I go, 'Well, fine, but for my industry, the global speaking one, he's fantastic.' Why? He's friendly, he's easy to work with, he's not greedy, he's a good speaker although he'll speak in French and you can translate. He'll do selfies.

Kenyon-Slaney chuckles to himself at this new development before he continues.

> And he'll say yes to things. So this year, for example, I've had him in Kazakhstan, I've had him in Iraq, I've had him in Angola, I've had him in Dubai. So what the clients are buying there is not François Hollande's record, they're buying someone who's been President of France, and it's a very important difference. You're buying into something bigger. Internationally, people very, very quickly forget crap records – of everyone. They can't remember. But when you see François Hollande, President of France, they see the important country.

Kenyon-Slaney tells me that the visit to Angola was about six weeks earlier, so it's fresh in his mind.

> I went to see him in his office. A former President has a very nice

office on the Rue de Rivoli. And what's so nice about going to France is he's just sitting there in his office having lunch. He sees three people now – intellectuals, journalists and MPs, basically. The deputies will go off, and then left around his office are half-open bottles of claret. I'm not suggesting they had a lot, but they had a bit. So you settle down in a chair with him, and he said to me, 'Tom, I'm going off to Angola for the event of the Global Tourism Forum. What am I going to speak about?' I said, 'Monsieur Le Président, France is one of the great centres of tourism, just talk about tourism in France, and they'll love it.' And off he went and did it. So the smart ones are versatile, the really clever ones, and Hollande would be a good example of that.

But if Ex Men like Hollande – or May – might overcome their records by virtue of having run a major country, what of those who ran small countries? Kenyon-Slaney represents quite a few of those too, including several of those I've spoken to for this book. And so I ask about one of them: Helen Clark. 'My observation about Helen is that she's the real deal in terms of a politician who really cares about society, and that's her passion. She's not commercially minded at all, she really is not bothered about doing any gigs,' he laughs.

She would like to, but we actually do very little because she's always turning them down. I think she's somebody who really knows what her vocation is, to try and make the world a better place, and wants to make herself available to everyone who she can help on that road.

There's a pause. 'It's interesting that you pick up on her, because I'd say she is someone who knows what she wants.' At the current count, Kenyon-Slaney represents twenty-four Ex Men; he bids for many more (including Blair, Cameron and May, all of whom ended up signing with different agencies), and so he sees a lot of them at a pivotal moment: the point when Jack McConnell was changing the start-up message on his mobile phone, the point when they're trying to console themselves and figure out what to do next. They come to him because, as he puts it, they see paid speaking as 'low-hanging fruit, and my insight with them is that they definitely see speaking as part of their core earnings. They've always done a lot of speaking themselves, they're quite good at it, unpaid obviously, and it's something they can turn their hand to very easily.' But when they get beyond the speaking, Kenyon-Slaney often finds a vacuum.

> My experience now of having worked with the top guys for a long time is a lot of them don't really know what to do when they step down from power. It actually amazes me how few seem to have real passions. Their passion seems to have been politics; they're a bit lost. And they're like, 'What do we do? Oh, let's do some speaking, let's do some advisory, let's write a book, let's set up a foundation, let's get on the board of a bank.' So one of the observations has always been that I find it actually quite disappointing that they don't really seem to have a plan post-politics.

American Presidents tend to have made plans, because the funds to build those libraries won't raise themselves. Tony Blair, of course, too, and some of the others who leave office only to take on major international jobs. As for the rest, I'm not sure I find it quite so disappointing as Kenyon-Slaney. I'm quite pleased to hear that until the moment they leave, our Prime Ministers and Presidents are focusing on the job of running the country rather than worrying about what they'll do afterwards. But I take his point, including a despair at the lack of other interests. Anyway, the reason Kenyon-Slaney has these conversations is that he and his London Speaker Bureau also support speakers, including many Ex Men, who want to find some advisory work, or a directorship or two. It's a hugely controversial area, and insofar as we in the media cover the lives of Ex Men, the focus is often on this side of the ledger. And it always comes with a side order of cynicism – what state secrets are they giving away to this hedge fund, what phone calls are they making on behalf of this bank, or what part of their soul are they selling to this oil company? This is largely the narrative about Ex Men; digging beneath it to see what else is going on has been part of my motivation for writing this book. And I think it's pretty clear from this book that many Ex Men are busy and active, on behalf of causes and issues and organisations which sometimes have a real effect on our lives. But that still leaves the question of the money. Are they selling a part of their souls for it, or tarnishing the office they once held, as is so often charged?[8] It perhaps won't surprise you to hear that the answer I've heard most often is 'no'. In a 2007 interview with *The Guardian*, for example, John Major, who has been sharply criticised over the years for his role at the Carlyle Group, a huge private equity firm at one time heavily invested in arms companies, was keen to emphasise the bright red line he drew between what he was, and wasn't, prepared to do. 'I advised them on what was going on around the world,' he told John Harris. 'I would represent them, I would do a whole range of things – but I would *not* lobby for them, and I did not introduce them to people. That was never my role, and I always made that perfectly clear.'[9]

Beyond that 'no', though, what are they up to? The answer is interesting, and it varies quite widely. Here's what Kim Campbell had to say on the subject when I'd just started the research for this book:

If you're smart enough to have been Prime Minister, chances are you have some leadership abilities that are valuable. I've sat on corporate boards. I never sat on corporate boards that paid me a huge amount of money – but I'm a good strategic thinker, and I was rewarded for it. I charge a lot of money for my consulting. I have a philosophy: I don't work for free for people that can afford to pay me, because I give an enormous amount of my time for nothing.

For years afterwards, I wondered about what she'd said: is she really a good strategic thinker, I asked myself, or was that the story she was telling herself? I kind of assumed that the companies she consulted for were really more interested in her contacts, or in having an association with a former Prime Minister. Malcolm Fraser has said as much about the approaches he received from companies.[10] But then I spoke to Paul Martin, Campbell's successor but one, whose career had been the reverse of hers; he'd reached the top of Canada's corporate ladder before quitting to enter politics. And he told me a story from that earlier part of his life, when a politician was being considered to join a board of which he was a member. 'I remember saying, "What do you want this person for? This is a business. What are they going to bring?" And they said, "They're going to bring some insights that we don't have." And I remember I was amazed at the breadth of knowledge that this person brought.' So far, so unsurprising, but Martin then took aim at one of the more popularly held beliefs about what Ex Men get up to when they're hired by the private sector.

I think that corporations who bring political figures on a board because they think they're going to give them contacts, they're making a hell of a mistake, because I don't think it works. But corporations who bring politicians on the board because they're going to give a perspective that other board directors, who've never been in public life, don't have – they're making a really good decision. Public life gives you a perspective on the world, and an understanding of current events, that businesspeople can never have. It always strikes me as strange that governments understand the need to reach out to academia or to business or to journalism because you have a perspective perhaps we don't have and we'd like to talk to you; and business thinks that the business of running the state doesn't give you a perspective that no one else has. It's childish, to be quite honest.

Set against that was a conversation I had with a very senior business leader who has hired several Ex Men over the years. He agreed with Paul Martin about using their contacts: none of the people he'd hired had ever brought in a single deal, he told me, and nor were they expected to. So what were they there for, I asked. The answer, when it came, was mundane and deflating: he'd hired these Ex Men, on their multi-million-pound salaries, to entertain his high-rolling clients. Essentially, when you're pitching for a billion-dollar contract, spending half a million dollars a year to hire a former Prime Minister or President to sit around the dinner table with your potential client is excellent value if it lands you the deal. Perhaps this is what John Major meant by representing a firm as opposed to lobbying for them, I wondered? Anyway, several years after this conversation I ask Tom Kenyon-Slaney, with all his experience of helping Ex Men find these kinds of advisory roles, whether it can really be true. Are Ex Men in the strategic advice business, or the hospitality trade? Are they serious advisers, or cherries on the top of a cake?

It's 95 per cent cherry. They just don't have the skills; a lot of them simply don't understand the corporate world. Occasionally there is a politician who has those skills. A very good one would be Fredrik Reinfeldt from Sweden, who's got those kind of advisory skills – a very thoughtful, intelligent, smart guy.

He mentions Toomas Ilves, too, a former Estonian President with very specific knowledge of the international tech scene. But in general? 'They are there to impress clients, they're there to draw people in.'

• • •

'My accumulated earnings would not serve me or my family adequately, so what were the areas that I could most appropriately do?' Joe Clark is talking me through his thinking about how he decided to earn money after serving as Prime Minister of Canada. The Canadians are good case studies because there's very little financial provision for them after they leave office, other than their parliamentary pension. Not every country even has that: Poland, for example, only introduced a presidential pension after Lech Wałęsa, in a brilliant stunt, turned up at the Gdansk shipyards, where he'd worked before he was elected President, and asked for his old electrician's job back.[11] But what about office support? Surely Clark must receive a lot of letters – doesn't he have any support for dealing with them, in the way that Ex Men in Britain, France, the United States and many others do? 'There's no support for that in Canada.' Do they expect you to sit at home each night replying to the day's mail or email? 'The volume declines as time passes, and I tend to regard that as an instrument of connection more than an obligation.' And then Clark pauses. 'I was elected several times in a rural constituency, including communities with relatively low incomes. I understand the scepticism of people in public life, I don't consider it unjustified.'

Fair enough, so what did he do to earn money? 'The immediate response was related to teaching, and to an academic role, and I did that a couple of times.' He also does some paid speaking, he says, and sits on some boards.

I was then approached by people who knew me, people not of my party, which was interesting, and asked to become associated in a consulting role with the combination of a national accounting firm and law firm. The understanding was that if there was an opportunity that I considered inappropriate, I could decline that, and I did that.

You declined things because they were inappropriate?

I have stayed away from things because I thought they were inappropriate. And you're never entirely sure about those judgements, but you're also aware that what you do is more likely to be scrutinised sometime than others. And I didn't want to be involved with something I thought would be inappropriate.

There is a prurient element to this discussion of what Ex Men do to earn money once they're out of office and the public are no longer paying their salaries. If politics is showbusiness for ugly people, as the old adage has it, this is, in part, the stuff of gossip columns. But I think it would be wrong to say it doesn't matter. After all, while the Canadian public may not be paying for Joe Clark, many other countries' taxpayers are still paying for security details, salaries, pensions and office costs. And despite what Tom Kenyon-Slaney told me about the Ex Men arriving at his door with no idea of what they want to do next, what little academic discussion there is of the role of Ex Men often focuses on the question of whether planning for future employment opportunities could affect a President's or Prime Minister's behaviour in office. And then there's the matter of decency. Different countries around the world handle these issues very differently, and many of the more thoughtful Ex Men with whom I've discussed them have expressed discomfort with what some of their colleagues have got up to. At various points they've expressed disapproval of John Major's relationship with the Carlyle Group, for example, or how they think Tony Blair has allowed the lines to blur between business and diplomacy. They've told me that they would find it personally embarrassing to be caught in those positions – 'cashing in', one called it. But they've also said they feel a responsibility not to shame or embarrass the office they once held. Jack McConnell, with whom I spoke very shortly after he left office, told me that he was mindful of the precedents he would set, and that he needed to be careful 'in the way I conduct myself privately and publicly, the tasks that I take on'. And that's because, for all that these are *Ex* Men, they are for ever shaped by the offices they once held. I think the person who put this best is Vaira Vīķe-Freiberga. 'The moral obligation to your country and the wish not to disgrace it publicly, as it were, that stays with you all your life,' she told me. 'I often said in Latvia in meeting people that I felt I had taken on the mantle of office, and then when I leave I just take the mantle off. That is not really 100 per cent true. There is a sort of tail which drags behind you.'

• • •

That's what this book has been about. About how this elite group, these Ex Men, use their superpowers to make the case for the liberal, democratic, international world order they helped establish while they were running it. But superpowers or not, these Ex Men are still that – Exes. And they need to reconcile themselves to that. Of all the people I've spoken to, perhaps Kim Campbell put it best. Campbell is not short of opinions, and in recent years she's become more vocal in sharing them – at one point having to apologise for a tweet suggesting she'd like to see a hurricane which was heading towards Florida flatten President Trump's Mar-a-Lago resort. But she's clear where the lines of responsibility lie for Ex Men. 'I wouldn't want to see a world where a group of former leaders came together and somehow had power to make things happen,' she told me, before she went on to outline what we can call 'The Campbell Rule'.

> I'd like to see a world where groups of former world leaders come together and address issues, and perhaps stand for things, advocate for things. But understanding that they're advocating in the same way that NGOs or any other group advocates, that we're not in power any more, and that hopefully our opinions might be valuable because of where they come from, but understanding that the responsibility to act is still with us as citizens and with those leaders that have the responsibility, and that our goal is to support good decision-making.

But in the course of researching and writing this book – interviewing two dozen Ex Men and hearing another two dozen speak – it's become quite clear to me that the Campbell Rule gets broken regularly. I hope it's clear to you, too: that groups of Ex Men come together and make things happen all the time. Because their superpowers don't desert them when they leave office. All the drive, ambition, passion, luck, all the personal relationships and lessons learned the hard way follow them out of the door, to be repurposed for their new roles, in their new lives. And this all matters because in their new lives they continue to change the world.

NOTES

INTRODUCTION

1 Rob Cameron, 'Art mirrors life in new Havel play', BBC News, 22 May 2008. The play deals with the transfer of power from one generation to another, and Havel describes the idea behind it in his memoir, *To the Castle and Back*, trans. Paul Wilson (London: Portobello Books, 2008): 'The interesting thing is that I started writing this play before the revolution, that is, sixteen years ago, and then I tossed the manuscript away in the belief that after all the changes taking place, the theme would no longer interest me. And then, having seen so many politicians around me who could not come to terms with the fact that they no longer held office, I began to return to it in my mind...', pp. 251–2.

2 Theresa May, 'Nationalism is no ally in this battle without borders', *The Times*, 6 May 2020.

3 'Tony Blair is having a Covid moment', *The Economist*, 30 April 2020.

4 Mary Robinson, *Everybody Matters: A Memoir* (London: Hodder & Stoughton, 2013), p. 6.

5 Sarah Sands, 'What the Prime Minister did next', *Evening Standard*, 27 June 2012.

6 "'I only do this job to help people": Under-fire Brown's emotive message to Labour rebels', *Evening Standard*, 17 April 2008.

7 'The 2008 Time 100', http://content.time.com/time/specials/packages/completelist/0,29569,1733748, 00.html

8 Andrew Jack, quoted in Kevin Theakston and Jouke de Vries (eds), *Former Leaders in Modern Democracies: Political Sunsets* (Basingstoke: Palgrave, 2012), p. 2.

9 Most notably Francis Beckett, David Hencke and Nick Kochan's book *Blair Inc.: The Man Behind the Mask* (London: John Blake, 2015).

10 Quoted in Kenneth P. Vogel, 'Chelsea flagged "serious concerns" about Clinton Foundation conflicts', Politico.com, 11 October 2016.

11 Alex Perry, 'Inside the Mind of Tony Blair: The Newsweek Interview', *Newsweek*, 10 April 2015.

12 Tony Blair, *A Journey* (London: Hutchinson, 2010).

CHAPTER 1: HISTORY

1 Douglas Brinkley, *The Unfinished Presidency: Jimmy Carter's Journey Beyond the White House* (New York: Viking, 1998), pp. 96–8.

2 Nancy Gibbs and Michael Duffy, *The Presidents Club: Inside the World's Most Exclusive Fraternity* (New York: Simon & Schuster, 2012), p. 440.

3 Iwan Morgan, 'After the White House: The Modern US Post-Presidency', in Kevin Theakston and Jouke de Vries (eds), *Former Leaders in Modern Democracies*, p. 23.

4 'A Day of Cameras and Hammers for Ex-President', *New York Times*, 4 September 1984, p. B03.

5 Five former Prime Ministers have become President of the Commission, three have become Presidents of the Council, and a further eight have become Commissioners.

6   Malcolm Fraser and Margaret Simons, *Malcolm Fraser: The Political Memoirs* (Carlton: Miegunyah Press, 2010), p. 1.
7   Ibid., p. 612.
8   Ibid., p. 635.
9   Sola Akinrinade, 'An army of ex-presidents: transitions, the military and democratic consolidation in Nigeria', in Roger Southall and Henning Melber (eds), *Legacies of Power: Leadership Change and Former Presidents in African Politics* (Cape Town: HSRC Press, 2006).
10 Malcolm Fraser and Margaret Simons, *Malcolm Fraser*, p. 671.

CHAPTER 2: CLUBS

1   Quoted in Gerald Ford, 'Personal Reflections on My Experiences as a Former President', in Richard Norton Smith and Timothy Walch, *Farewell to the Chief: Former Presidents in American Public Life* (Worland: High Plains Publishing Co. Inc., 1990), p. 173.
2   Jimmy Carter, 'Losing My Religion for Equality', *Sydney Morning Herald*, 15 July 2009.
3   Austin Ruse, 'Global Gallivanting Gasbags Who Refuse to Leave the Stage', Breitbart.com, 5 May 2015.
4   Alex Vines, 'Elite Bargains and Political Deals Project: Mozambique Case Study', Stabilisation Unit, February 2018, https://assets.publishing.service.gov.uk/government/uploads/system/uploads/attachment_data/file/766037/Mozambique_case_study.pdf
5   The club's website says 'around thirty': http://www.clubmadrid.org/policy-dialogue/2013/

CHAPTER 3: THE CAMPAIGNER

1   Gerald Ford and Jimmy Carter, 'A Time to Heal Our Nation', *New York Times*, 21 December 1998.
2   Fernando Henrique Cardoso with Brian Winter, *The Accidental President of Brazil: A Memoir* (New York: PublicAffairs, 2006).
3   '"It's a lie": former Japanese prime minister Junichiro Koizumi blasts Shinzo Abe's government over Fukushima clean-up', *South China Morning Post*, 8 September 2016.
4   Takashi Arichika, 'Koizumi says Japan must say "no" to nuclear energy', *Asahi Shimbun*, 17 January 2019.
5   John Major, *John Major: The Autobiography* (London: HarperCollins, 1999).
6   Greg Heffer, '"Trashing their reputations": Fury as Blair and Major claim Brexit would destroy "UK unity"', *Daily Express*, 9 June 2016.
7   Isaac Chotiner, 'Gordon Brown's case for global cooperation during the coronavirus pandemic', *New Yorker*, 18 April 2020.
8   Gaby Hinsliff, 'Gordon Brown on Covid-19, recession and Trump: "When there's a crisis you have to act quickly"', *The Guardian*, 16 April 2020.
9   Quoted in Francis Beckett and Mark Seddon, *Jeremy Corbyn and the Strange Rebirth of Labour England* (London: Biteback Publishing, 2018), p. 198.

CHAPTER 4: THE SPECIALIST

1   Tony Blair, *A Journey*, p. 516.
2   Eleanor Ainge Roy, 'Helen Clark: WHO coronavirus inquiry aims to "stop the world being blindsided again"', *The Guardian*, 10 July 2020.

CHAPTER 5: THE LEADER

1   Mary Robinson, *Everybody Matters*.
2   Kevin Boyle, Introduction in Kevin Boyle (ed.), *A Voice For Human Rights: Mary Robinson* (Philadelphia: University of Pennsylvania Press, 2007).
3   Kevin Theakston, 'Former Prime Minister in Britain since 1945', in Kevin Theakston and Jouke de Vries (eds), *Former Leaders in Modern Democracies*, p. 44.

CHAPTER 6: THE DIPLOMAT

1 Lieven De Winter and Ilona Rezsöhazy, 'The Afterlives of Belgian Prime Ministers', in Kevin Theakston and Jouke de Vries (eds), *Former Leaders in Modern Democracies*, p. 207.

CHAPTER 7: CONSCIENCE

1 Ivor Porter, *Michael of Romania: The King and the Country* (Cheltenham: Sutton Publishing, 2005).
2 Quoted in ibid., p. 205.
3 Tony Barber, 'Turkey needs to "upgrade" its democracy, says former president', *Financial Times*, 28 October 2015.
4 'Turkish former president says country was wrong to adopt presidential system', Ahval, 18 February 2020.
5 Murat Yetkin, 'Will former President Gul start a new party?' *Hürriyet Daily News*, 5 December 2016.
6 'Ex-President of Turkey, former Erdogan allies to form new rival party', *Middle East Monitor*, 27 June 2019.
7 'Babacan loses key ally Gül as he forms new Turkish political party', Ahvalnews.com, 9 March 2020.
8 Ellen Lutz and Caitlin Reiger, 'Introduction', in Ellen Lutz (ed.), *Prosecuting Heads of State* (Cambridge: Cambridge University Press, 2009), p. 2.
9 Daniel Hoffman, 'Despot deposed: Charles Taylor and the challenge of state reconstruction in Liberia', in Roger Southall and Henning Melber, *Legacies of Power*, p. 314.
10 Ibid., p. 309.
11 Ellen Lutz and Caitlin Reiger, 'Introduction', p. 4.
12 Ibid., p. 11.

CHAPTER 8: BRAND EX

1 David Remnick, 'The Wanderer', *New Yorker*, 18 September 2006.
2 Iwan Morgan, 'After the White House: The Modern US Post-Presidency', p. 28.
3 Daniel Halper, *Clinton, Inc.: The audacious rebuilding of a political machine* (New York: Broadside Books, 2014), p. 106.
4 Epitomised by Halper's book.
5 Quoted in David Remnick, 'The Wanderer'.
6 John Daniel, 'Soldiering on: the post-presidential years of Nelson Mandela 1995–2005', in Roger Southall and Henning Melber, *Legacies of Power*, p. 26.
7 Ibid., p. 29.
8 Jeffrey M. Jones, 'Obama, Trump Tie as Most Admired Man in 2019', Gallup, 30 December 2019.
9 Kate Andersen Brower, 'Trump's Cold War with the Former Presidents', *Vanity Fair*, April 2020.
10 Ibid.

CHAPTER 9: THE LAST STAND

1 Václav Havel, *To the Castle and Back*, pp. 14–15.
2 Sir John Major, *Between Ourselves*, BBC Radio 4, 4 September 2008.
3 Richard Spears, 'The History of Presidential Libraries', in 'White House History: The Presidential Libraries', *Journal of the White House Historical Association*, no. 40, 2016, p. 11.
4 Douglas Brinkley, quoted in Iwan Morgan, 'After the White House: The Modern US Post-Presidency', p. 17.
5 Fernando Henrique Cardoso, *The Accidental President of Brazil: A Memoir*; George Bush and Brent Scowcroft, *A World Transformed* (New York: Vintage, 1998).

6   *When the Power's Switched Off*, BBC Radio 4, 21 April 2007, produced by Martin Rosenbaum.

7   Roger Southall, Neo Simutanyi and John Daniel, 'Former presidents in African politics', in Roger Southall and Henning Melber, *Legacies of Power*, p. 1.

8   A good example is Todd Purdum, 'The Comeback Id', *Vanity Fair*, July 2008, on Bill Clinton's post-presidency.

9   John Harris, 'Into the Void', *Guardian Weekend*, 3 February 2007.

10 Malcolm Fraser and Margaret Simons, *Malcolm Fraser*, pp. 612–14.

11 The story is relayed in Kevin Theakston and Jouke de Vries (eds), *Former Leaders in Modern Democracies*, p. 6.

FURTHER READING

There are disappointingly few books about Ex Men, and they tend to fall into one of two categories: academic overviews, or books about the American post-presidency. They vary in quality, but a few stand out.

The Presidents Club: Inside the World's Most Exclusive Fraternity, by Nancy Gibbs and Michael Duffy, is an excellent guide to relationships between former Presidents and their successors, and in my opinion the best of the books about the US post-presidency. It's extremely interesting, very well sourced and very readable.

After Number 10: Former Prime Ministers in British Politics, by Kevin Theakston, is a comprehensive academic overview of what every British Prime Minister has done after leaving office.

Former Leaders in Modern Democracies: Political Sunsets, edited by Kevin Theakston and Jouke de Vries, is another academic overview, but more analytical and covering a much wider range of countries: the US and UK, but also Canada, Australia, Germany, France, Ireland, the Netherlands, Belgium and Israel.

Legacies of Power: Leadership Change and Former Presidents in African Politics, edited by Roger Southall and Henning Melber, provides very helpful description and analysis of a number of African countries, including Botswana, Zambia, Namibia, Malawi, Uganda,

Kenya, Ghana, Nigeria and Liberia, as well as more focused chapters on the post-presidencies of Nelson Mandela, Julius Nyerere and one asking why Robert Mugabe would not leave office (published before he did).

ACKNOWLEDGEMENTS

I've been writing this book for more than ten years. That is a long time to be working on anything, which means two things. First, a lot of people have helped me get this book published. And second, a few people have given me a lot of space to do it.

First and most obviously, I am enormously grateful to all the Ex Men who have spoken to me for this book. All of them lead busy lives, and in choosing to answer my questions they've opened themselves up to a scrutiny which is no longer an obligation. Thank you, too, to all the people who have facilitated these interviews – their partners, assistants, press people and former employees. And a similar thank-you to all the people who have spoken to me about the Ex Men – many on the record, many not – without whom this book would be just a collection of interviews. Two organisations – the InterAction Council and the Global Leadership Foundation – placed sufficient trust in this project, and me, to allow me access to their annual meetings, so I wish to record my thanks to them in particular. And I'm likewise grateful to the press teams at Chatham House, the London School of Economics and King's College London, who have made available seats to countless events with Ex Men over the past decade.

Ten years is a long time to have a side project on the go, and I am grateful for the forbearance of my many fantastic colleagues at the BBC. The person who has put up with most is Martin Rosenbaum, who has probably heard me suggest one Ex Man or another as a potential interviewee for more or less every documentary he has worked on throughout this time, and always smiled! He has also proved a source of wise counsel and generous advice. The same is true for Jane Ashley, Peter Snowdon, Jonathan Brunert, Leala Padmanabhan, Rob Shepherd, Daniel Kraemer, Patrick Cowling, Ben Wright, Rajini Vaidyanathan, Philippa Thomas, Malcolm Balen, Nick Robinson, James Naughtie, Emma Barnett, Chris Hunter, Mohit Bakaya, Richard Knight, Steve Titherington, Matthew Dodd, Gwyneth Williams, Mary Hockaday, Ann Gardiner, Richard Townsend, Hal Haines and Sue Inglish. All of them have offered helpful suggestions and been valuable sounding boards for my ideas about this book over the years. Similarly, many of the non-BBC friends with whom I've had the privilege of working have offered tremendously helpful thoughts and comments, in particular Steven Rahman, Phil Cowley, Shaharazad Abuel-Ealeh, Stephen Ostrowski, Mary Ann Sieghart, Byron Vincent, Matthew Taylor, Farrah Jarral and Sayeeda Warsi. All of them have helped this book, but if there are any errors or omissions they are, of course, mine alone.

As I write in the book, I first became interested in these questions at the Harvard Kennedy School, and the drive to Oakland at the end of my year there, with the brilliant Hilary Weinstein, really cemented it. I'm so grateful she gave up a trip through potentially more exciting cities to hang out in presidential libraries instead (and for her pains nearly got swept up in a tornado to boot), and for her friendship since. Likewise, Peter Hennessy, instrumental in me spending that year in America, has been a friend and mentor for more than twenty years now and has supported this project from the start.

Thanks, too, to everyone at Biteback, but in particular to Namkwan Cho for the fantastic cover design and to my editor Olivia Beattie, who has supported this project from the start, stuck with it for ten years, and I hope she is pleased (and will certainly be relieved) that it has finally come to fruition: thank you, Olivia.

Finally, the people without whom this really wouldn't have been possible are my family. This book is dedicated to my parents, whose unconditional love and support throughout everything I have done in my life has been astonishing, sustaining and life-affirming. I am overwhelmingly grateful to my wonderful wife Vinita, whose question opened this book, for always asking the question which makes me think again; not to mention making space for me to research and write it. But the people who have made the largest sacrifice, who have been my biggest distraction – and the best anyone could hope for – are my daughters, Maya and Leela. They are a source of immense joy in my life, and now that this is finished, I hope we'll be able to spend much more time together.

Giles Edwards
August 2020

INDEX